PRAISE FOR AS A WOMAN

"This book is nothing less than an audacious, gripping, and profoundly real journey that speaks to the mind, heart, and soul. As we grapple with what it means to love people as Jesus did, *As a Woman* provides poignant insights into the beauty, complexity, and deeply intersectional nature of all God's children. What's more, Paula's brilliant writing, discerning reflections, and incisive wit make this an important and accessible read. It will teach you lessons about loving yourself, God, and others—and challenge you in all the right ways."

—Joshua J. Dickson, director of faith-based
initiatives, Biden campaign

"Powerfully and tenderly written with a poetic flair, *As a Woman* is in the end surprisingly practical for anyone ready to examine their own presuppositions about faith, power, sexuality, and gender."

—Joe Boyd, co-founder and CEO, Rebel Pilgrim

"The only thing more emotional than reading about Paula's unceremonious severing from her job after coming out as transgender is following along in awe as Paula took those shattered pieces and showed that death truly does not have the last word. And while her story inspires us to live for the truth of who we are, it is her unique insights into the differences between living as a man and a woman that empower us to live for the greater good of all. What Paula has done in *As a Woman* is magnificent."

—Colby Martin, author of *UnClobber: Rethinking our Misuse of the Bible on Homosexuality*, and co-pastor/founder of Sojourn Grace Collective, San Diego

"*As a Woman* is a heart-rending and brave spiritual memoir of gender transition. Reading Paula Stone Williams, I wept then understood; felt angry then empowered. This book is ultimately about the joyful triumph of an authentic and faithful life, a profoundly human and humane story of love and justice."

—Diana Butler Bass, author of *Freeing Jesus:*
Rediscovering Jesus as Friend, Teacher,
Savior, Lord, Way, and Presence

"*As a Woman* is a masterful and unflinching story that will challenge the ways in which you see the world, other people, and even yourself. Anyone on a journey of discovery will feel at home in Paula's book."

—Katrina Mathewson, screenwriter and co-chair
of the Writers Guild of America's
LGBTQ+ Committee

"Perhaps no human experience is as misunderstood today as that of the transgender person. That means we are called to listen and learn—first from transgender people themselves. I pray the world may begin to pay attention to the stories of people like Paula, and open our hearts to their struggles, concerns, and dreams."

—James Martin, SJ, author of *Building a Bridge*

"Paula's book is an essential read for any human who takes seriously their obligation to help close the gender equity gap. If understanding is the first step to action, then reading what Paula has to say about succeeding on both sides is the best place to start."

—Cindy W. Anderson, global lead,
Engagement & Eminence,
IBM Institute for Business Value

"*As a Woman*, at its simplest, is a story about bravery and what it takes to follow one's heart and authentic self despite the consequences. The impact of Paula's transition is palpable as she details losing the power, privilege, and prestige that came with being an evangelical pastor, a successful CEO, and a man. However, it is through Paula's unique lens—her life experiences on both sides—that she is able to so acutely pinpoint the realities of gender bias."

—Caitie Bradley Shea, CEO,
Outspoken Agency

"Fired, robbed, disowned, and dismissed by the evangelical Christian world in which she once rose to power, Paula could have become bitter. But instead she chose to become better—more thoughtful, more understanding, more self-reflective, more conscious of other people's lives. Hers is a spiritual journey worth joining."

—Linda Kay Klein, author of *Pure: Inside the Evangelical Movement that Shamed a Generation of Young Women and How I Broke Free*

"Paula is one of the most courageous individuals you'll find. Her wisdom is expansive yet graceful, and her story reveals an authentic journey that we can all learn from. In the end, she reminds us that at the heart of everything is love."

—Jeremy Duhon, curator,
TEDxMileHigh

AS A WOMAN

WHAT I LEARNED ABOUT
POWER, SEX, AND THE PATRIARCHY
AFTER I TRANSITIONED

Paula Stone Williams

ATRIA BOOKS

New York • London • Toronto • Sydney • New Delhi

ATRIA
BOOKS

An Imprint of Simon & Schuster, Inc.
1230 Avenue of the Americas
New York, NY 10020

First Atria Books hardcover edition June 2021

ATRIA BOOKS and colophon are trademarks of Simon & Schuster, Inc.

For information about special discounts for bulk purchases, please contact Simon & Schuster Special Sales at 1-866-506-1949 or business@simonandschuster.com.

The Simon & Schuster Speakers Bureau can bring authors to your live event. For more information or to book an event, contact the Simon & Schuster Speakers Bureau at 1-866-248-3049 or visit our website at www.simonspeakers.com.

Interior design by Dana Sloan

Manufactured in the United States of America

1   3   5   7   9   10   8   6   4   2

Library of Congress Cataloging-in-Publication Data
Names: Williams, Paula Stone, author.
Title: As a woman : what I learned about power, sex, and the patriarchy after I transitioned / Paula Stone Williams.
Description: First edition. | New York : Atria Books, 2021.
Identifiers: LCCN 2020058146 (print) | LCCN 2020058147 (ebook) | ISBN 9781982153342 (hardcover) | ISBN 9781982153366 (ebook)
Subjects: LCSH: Williams, Paula Stone. | Male-to-female Transsexuals—United States—Biography. | Clergy—United States—Biography. | Christian transgender people—Family relationships.
Classification: LCC HQ77.8.W55 A3 2021 (print) | LCC HQ77.8.W55 (ebook) | DDC 306.76/8—dc23
LC record available at https://lccn.loc.gov/2020058146
LC ebook record available at https://lccn.loc.gov/2020058147

ISBN 978-1-9821-5334-2
ISBN 978-1-9821-5336-6 (ebook)

For All Who Believe Living Authentically Is
Sacred and Holy and for the Greater Good

Contents

PART III

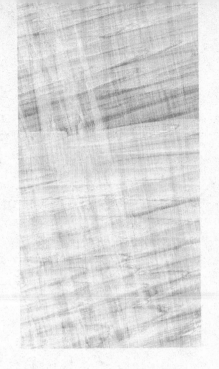

AS A WOMAN

What You Write This For

This is a poem written for me by my friend Nicole Kelly Vickey at the start of writing this book, as a reminder of what I was writing it for.

Don't write it for the money,
or just to feel known,
because this won't feel like that.
It will feel more like pouring out
your soul to an empty room.
Responses will come at odd intervals,
and often from the people hit the hardest.
I've read so many authors
who have brought me to tears,
to a fundamental understanding of some corner of myself.
And I never, ever
wrote one a letter to tell them so or say thank you.
Be wary of wrapping up story lines that aren't finished yet.

Hold space for new chapters in new books.
You don't know yet where this will all lead,
or how you will fit again into some
future iteration of a friendship
that once felt like it kept you alive
but right now feels a bit like a dead end.
Write it for the souls out there
behind you on a similar path.
The ones who feel like
they were born somehow wrong,
who need the map of what it took for you to set things right.
Those who are growing under a broken parent,
who learn how to be loved by studying others
who've also had to learn that for themselves.
Those who find themselves stuck in marriages
that have grown to fit all wrong,
and yet are still the most comfortable thing they know.
Those who feel pressed into careers,
but have to name them callings.
Those who give their whole hearts
to causes which consume them and shut the door.
Pour out the blood of your story
so that one day
down some dusty library row
the right reader will find you,
take you home,
ink up your margins
with notes like "this is me,"
read you in their bath,
hold you in their hands

as the tears they don't show anyone else
blur your pages
though you will never meet,
or know their names,
or how your words ineffably changed them.

Trusting the Flow

It's never too late to be what you might have been.

—GEORGE ELIOT

I had a big dream but could not hold on to the details, except some vague sense that I'd been immersed in water. As I stared at the ceiling, all I could feel was the dream's heft, pregnant and profound. A week or so later the dream returned, focused on the water in my backyard, water that returns to itself as it falls and swirls over boulders and stones. The water is stuck in a Sisyphean cycle, falling only to be pushed back up, moving swiftly but going nowhere.

I have to fill my backyard water feature every five or six days. Weary of its circular journey, the water gives up and evaporates. The babbling brook is not self-sustaining. It requires electricity to run the pump and a human to fill the basin. The water has to be handled. Rivers do not have to be handled. Rivers should be trusted.

I walk down from my house to the nearby St. Vrain River and its unfamiliar pathways, carved by a 2013 storm of biblical proportions. The river, more a stream most seasons, now meanders through fields where Black Angus once grazed. It makes its way into and out of its old riverbed, following the instructions of an ever-evolving Mother Nature. In spite of its new twists and turns, the river still knows where it is going. The river is going to the sea. The river is not stuck.

I was. Stuck, that is. I had been going through my own storm of biblical proportions and felt like the water in my backyard water feature, cascading down only to be forced back up. That was the essence of the dream as it returned, time and again.

About a month after the recurring dream began, I was visiting friends in New England. As the full moon cast its scattered shadow on an early spring snow, I sat by the fire with my friend Carol and talked of being caught in a never-ending cycle. She looked at the stuck me and said matter-of-factly, "You're stuck because you're trying to go back. You know you can't go back, right? Seriously, you know you can't go back. You have to let go and trust the flow."

I was not trusting my heart. I had spent decades resisting its flow, engineering results more acceptable to my upbringing. But they were Rube Goldberg creations, convoluted machinery that never could really stop the flow. But life provides opportunities for redemption, and eventually the slow work of God had brought me here, to this place of yielding, where I might trust the flow and its long and winding journey to the sea.

Nowadays people say, "You are so brave and courageous." I am one of the first transgender people they have ever known, and they want to express their admiration. I am touched, but for a long time I felt neither brave nor courageous. I allowed my charmed life to stop me from trusting my heart.

I was a successful White man, the son of an evangelical pastor, the CEO of a national ministry, a magazine editor and pastoral counselor. Because I was one of the leaders who controlled the agenda, I never had to give up a part of myself. When I went into a business meeting, I did not have to worry about how I was dressed, or the accent with which I spoke, or the language I used. Life was tailored to my needs. The world was made for my pleasure. Yet I was restless and depressed. When you stand in opposition to your heart's desire, you are going to feel restless and depressed. Your own soul is judging you.

My life was unfolding in opposition to my heart's desire. But life is ultimately generative, and requested or not, the soul does eventually rise up and cry out, "For God's sake, get a backbone!" That's what happened by the fire that snowy New England night. Carol's words sent me searching for my backbone. I found it where I had left it in a fit of fear, and it spoke with a voice I could not deny. I had been called.

The feeling in Carol's living room began in my gut and crept into my soul, burning hotter than the fire holding us in its embrace. My legs were crossed, and as my heart raced, my right foot moved ever so slightly with each throbbing beat. I couldn't take my eyes off of my foot, moving, restless, ready. My heart was demanding to be heard. I was being called to move, to leave the comfort of the meaningful life I was living and embrace the more dangerous life churning within. I was called to transition genders. Paul was to give way to Paula.

Was the call from God? Who knows? I do know it was from a place so deep it scared me—a place that had never been granted freedom. It came as a knowing of the heart, born of conviction, accompanied by enormous fear. It arrived with demands.

It is easier to live unaware, to get out of bed in the morning and leave your better half under the covers, ignoring the life you might have chosen if only you could have mustered the courage to choose it. It is easier to give up the terrifying possibility of freedom in exchange for the relative comfort of community, even if it is a community of people frightened of the wrath of the gods.

It was a decade ago that I took in the full measure of Carol's words as we sat around the warm fire. Afterward, I spent a great period of time lost, but it's all right, because lost is a place, too. Sometimes you have to spend a season or two there.

I offer no excuses. It takes a long time to answer the big questions. There are periods, sometimes years, when you just have to prepare dinner and put the kids to bed and finish the laundry and fix the blinds by the bay window that open crooked before you are finally free to take the road less traveled by. All the giant leaps do not have to come at once.

My heart spent decades preparing to receive its call. When it finally came, it took longer still to let go and trust the flow. Eventually, in fits and starts, I exploded the family narrative and shocked a whole denomination and transitioned from Paul to Paula. I lost all of my jobs and a lot of my money and most of my friends and stepped onto the road of trials with barely a clue what to do or where to go. Was I ready for this? No one is ready for the trauma of transitioning genders. No White man is prepared for the loss of privilege. But I had been called, so I listened to my heart and jumped in the water and hoped for the best, trusting that the river does know its way to the sea.

This is the story of my trip to the sea. We are all on a journey, maybe our first, maybe our last, but all into the unknown. But this living is serious business, and we are pilgrims, called by our better angels to live authentically. For all the uncertainty, we can know two things: the heart yearns to be free, but it will never *be* free until you let go of the world to which you no longer belong. Everything after that is a sacred and holy adventure.

PART I

CHAPTER 1

My Wedding Night

Opening his arms he said quietly to her, "Disappear here."

—JONATHAN CARROLL

A cold, hard rain was falling across the South Shore of Long Island. It had been pouring all day, through the Sunday-morning church service, the afternoon football game, and again as I drove the few blocks to the church late that evening. It was December 31, 1972, my wedding day. I was twenty-one. Cathy was nineteen. Her father had decided it would be marvelous to have our wedding ceremony at 11:30 p.m. and be announced as husband and wife shortly before midnight. And so, it was.

I was uneasy and had been since July. In my final summer between college semesters, I worked weekdays mowing the college-owned

13

cemetery, the one where my grandfather was buried, the one where my grandmother, mother and father, aunts, uncles, and cousin are now buried. As I carved patterns of grass across the open fields, I pondered a nagging question: *Why am I not more excited about getting married?* I knew I loved Cathy and wanted to start a family, but I also knew there were rumblings in my heart that were refusing to be bedded down. I couldn't name them. My head and heart weren't communicating very well. But like a brick of peat buried in ash, I knew there was a fire waiting to come to life.

September arrived and with it, my senior year of college. Cathy returned to campus after a summer at home in New York. I was busy working, going to school, and looking for a place to live and a second job to pay the rent. Late at night, spinning records at the radio station where I worked, I let my mind wander to the smoldering embers that lay beneath my busyness. *Why do I care so much about the flowers at our wedding, or the bridesmaids' dresses, or all the things other guys are not thinking about?*

One night, as Karen Carpenter sang, "I'm on the top of the world lookin' down on creation," I thought about how much I wanted to sing with the voice of Karen Carpenter—deep, resonant, and feminine. Later that same night, while sitting with nothing to do during a broadcast of a Cincinnati Reds game, I let my mind wander. *What if I were the bride and not the groom?* I thought about what it would be like to shop for a wedding dress and walk down the aisle. I got so caught up in the vision that I missed a station ID at the top of the hour. I stuffed the thought back into the depths of my soul.

As I drove to the church that rainy December night, dressed in my brown rented tux and too-tight pants, I was committed. I was getting married, and that was that. The building was fairly empty, and Steve, my friend who was playing keyboards, called me over to practice the medley of tunes I would be singing during the ceremony. My voice was uncharacteristically thin and unsure of itself. I hoped it would get stronger before the ceremony.

At 11:30, with my groomsmen behind me, I walked out the side door near the stage. My legs were shaking. The bridesmaids came down the aisle, one by one, and then as Steve played the opening chords of Wagner's "Bridal Chorus," everyone stood and Cathy came down the aisle, radiant and stunning. Suddenly I was confident and in love and sure all manner of things would be well. I sang a medley from a Johnny Mathis album that included the Carpenter's tune "We've Only Just Begun," and now my voice had the resonance it lacked a couple of hours earlier. The vows began, people prayed, the clock struck midnight, and it was 1973. Cathy and I were married.

As was the custom in my evangelical culture, a short reception with cake and punch followed in the church basement. Since it was well after midnight, the reception was even shorter than usual. As sheets of rain blew in from the Atlantic, the guests departed.

It was 3:30 a.m. before Cathy and I got to the hotel where we would spend our first night as a married couple. It was a Holiday Inn near the Long Island Expressway. We both went into the lobby and I told the receptionist I had a reservation for Paul and Cathy Williams. It felt wrong to have given Cathy my name. I felt barely old enough to own it myself. Yet I still felt the confidence I had felt as Cathy came down the aisle. I was proud she was my wife. I knew who I wanted to go to bed with. The question I was avoiding was who I wanted to go to bed as.

The receptionist handed me the key and Cathy and I walked down the empty hallway to a west-facing room on the second floor of the modest hotel. There was a gold carpet, and turquoise bedspreads on the two beds, each with a gold throw pillow. The room had one captain's chair on either side of a standing lamp, a dresser against the wall, and a television on a pedestal. There was no marriage suite, just carbon copy rooms with concrete ceilings, thick curtained windows, and all the charm you would expect of a Holiday Inn on an interstate.

Standing in the bathroom brushing my teeth, I stared at the mirror. I saw a kid, really, who still had pimples on his chin, there in a T-shirt and briefs, clueless. How had I gotten here? I left the bathroom and got into bed. Cathy crawled under the covers fifteen minutes later.

Even though it was after 4:00 a.m., we made love more than once. It was the first time either one of us had ever had sex, or even been that close to someone else's naked body. Our evangelical roots forbade premarital sex. All of our senses were far too overwhelmed to fully take in the splendor of that night. The feel of her body against mine, my fingers running through her hair, the whisper of her heart's affections into my ear, and the way my rough body responded to her soft touch. It was glorious, worth the wait, a tender time of youth.

After a few hours of restless sleep, I woke shortly after dawn. Cathy was in a deep sleep, lying on her side, hair cascading across the pillow. I could not believe I was lucky enough to have married someone as beautiful as Cathy. I had done well, marrying the most wonderful girl on campus. Suddenly, without invitation, a deep unease overwhelmed me. I was acutely aware of my body as I stared at the parallel lines in the creases of the white concrete ceiling. My dark hair, broad shoulders, stubble of beard, genitalia. Every cell was awake and on edge. My eyes focused on a single spot above the bed, where there were slight pockmarks in the concrete. There was a catch in my breath, and I whispered audibly, "Oh God, I'm in the wrong body."

CHAPTER 2

A Gender Revealed

The past is our definition. We may strive with good
reason to escape it, or to escape what is bad in it. But we
will escape it only by adding something better to it.

—WENDELL BERRY

Round Lake Christian Camp was my favorite summer retreat. I tagged along with my father, who led a senior-high week at the Ohio church camp every July. Once I was old enough to be trusted, I'd spend a good bit of each lazy afternoon rowing a boat from one side of the lake to the other. When you row a boat, you travel forward while facing backward, and I learned you can navigate pretty accurately by looking at the point where you began. I would row to my favorite spot on the far side of the lake, a tiny cove where I could sit and listen to the sounds coming across the water. Then, keeping my eyes fixed on a grassy rise to the left and a sugar maple to the right, I would row back to the dock without turning around more than once or twice. It was a good lesson, learning to travel forward while looking back. I felt independent, confident, proud, a twelve-year-old boy making his way across the lake, with a freedom available only to boys in those days. Girls were not allowed to row boats across lakes. Boys had better rules.

From my cozy spot in the tiny cove, I spent afternoons gazing across the lake at the teenagers living their important teenage lives, which all seemed to have something to do with the opposite sex. The allure of girls was beginning to awaken within, but I had more important things to do. My job was to daydream. I thought about the people on the other side of the lake, like the camp cook who would charitably fry the bluegill I caught that morning. I thought of the lifeguard who played jazz on the old camp piano. And there was his beautiful wife, who I secretly wanted to be. I thought a lot about that when I was sitting in my little cove. I loved watching his wife, the gentle way she held their young daughter, the way she moved around the campgrounds, soft and feminine. I liked the way boys deferred to her, and I secretly stole glances when she was in her bathing suit. I wanted to have her body and wear that bathing suit.

Eight years earlier, my family was living on Piedmont Road in Huntington, West Virginia. I distinctly remember being in the bathroom of the house thinking, *Before long I will have to decide whether to stand up or sit down when I go to the bathroom.* That was it. No great epiphany, just the thought that I would soon have to decide whether to be a boy or a girl. A simple thought with profound implications. Somehow, I had fashioned the notion that I got to choose my gender. I pictured a blond gender fairy dressed in powder blue, holding a white wand. With a gentle voice she would say, "Well, my dear, the time has come. Do you choose to be a boy or a girl?" I would answer and her wand would do its magic. When I think about it now, it was a pretty novel way for a transgender child to create a narrative that matched her desire.

I did not dislike being a boy. There were days I thought I might remain one. But there were far more days when I was sure I would tell the gender fairy I was a girl. From as early as I can remember, in my heart I longed to be a girl. I would imagine myself the sister of the girl next door, petite, cute, and feminine. I wanted to be like her.

The idea that I got to choose my gender was a sign of an already developing male entitlement. I had a brother four years older than I, but all of my cousins were girls. I got more of Grandma Stone's attention than any of the girls. I demanded it. The world told me I had a right to demand it. Boys got first pickings; the girls waited. Grandma Stone never sat down to eat a meal she had prepared until all the men and children had eaten. Then she would take her dinner in the kitchen. I was paying attention. The men sat in the parlor and talked about whether Adlai Stevenson could beat Ike Eisenhower. If one of the girls expressed an opinion, she was interrupted or ignored. If I had an opinion, I was allowed to speak. And yes, though I was only five, I knew who the candidates were, and I also knew most of my Kentucky family were Democrats. I was a novelty, encouraged in my precociousness. "Well, look at that. Little Paul knows who the candidates are."

I assumed I was special, because the world treated me that way. Why shouldn't I believe I got to choose my gender? It seemed like the kind of thing a boy would be empowered to do. Of course, I had no idea that if I had been able to choose my gender, every bit of privilege I was already enjoying would have disappeared. I did not realize a girl is given invisibility almost as a birthright, as my friend Carla puts it. It begins outside and moves inside, internalized for life, unless an extraordinary empowering grace intervenes.

I loved dressing as a girl, particularly when I was playing with my girl cousins. We would dress in my grandmother's old clothes, left for us to play with in the bedroom next to the back porch. I loved those playtimes. I knew they would not occur if I was alone at Grandma's, or there with Myron, my older brother. The clothes would not come out unless my cousins were there, and I longed for those occasions, not only for the chance to play dress-up, but also because I loved being with my cousins. Their play was gentler than the boys', more talking and less shouting and loud motor noises. We would play house and have tea parties and it made me giddy. That is, until that day.

I was five. I had lingered longer in the bedroom and was more daring than usual. I was in one of Grandma's blue dresses, stockings, and high-heeled shoes when my mother suddenly came into the room. Sternly, she demanded that I remove the clothes. What did I think I was doing? She shook her head disapprovingly, then used way too many words for way too long a time, telling me I had done something bad. Finally, she turned and walked away. No tender hug and a heartfelt "It's all right, Paul. I still love you." Just the back of my mother walking away as she returned to the kitchen. I heard her talking to her mother, saying nothing about what had just happened in the back bedroom. She acted like everything was just peachy. I was embarrassed and ashamed and ripped off the clothes, crying silently as I gave up my dreamy identity. I never forgot that encounter, and I never wore Grandma's clothes again.

Then, seven years later, I was sitting in a cove on the south side of Round Lake, daydreaming about the wife of the head lifeguard. As much as I longed to be a girl, I was finding my way as a boy and it was not awful. I was not the kind of transgender child who hates life and wants to die because God has not granted their wish to change genders. I had resigned myself to life as a boy. It was not what I wanted, but I thought I could live with it.

When you finally do find the courage to transition genders, enlightened people think they know your narrative. "Paula felt like a girl in a boy's body." For me, that was not true. I felt like a boy in a boy's body, and I didn't like it. I wished I had been born a girl. I felt I was supposed to have been born a girl.

My consistent longing was most present before I went to sleep and when I first woke up. It would often rear its head during the day, but it was not an everyday occurrence. After my traumatic encounter with my mother, I had determined I would never again wear my grandmother's clothes, or the clothes of any other girl. I would never again imagine myself as a girl. But of course, one's gender identity is neither a factor of will nor of genitalia. It is of the deep psyche, and like one's sexual identity, it is most likely fixed before birth. I was no more able to stop dressing in girls' clothes than I was able to stop breathing. That was why it was so satisfying to sit in my little cove on the far side of the lake and imagine myself as the wife of the lifeguard. I was keeping alive what I knew to be true. I was supposed to have been born a girl.

I used to go to bed at night gratefully tucked in by the adults who cared for me. They would tell me how special I was and pray with me. But as much as I trusted those people, I knew they would never be able to tell me who I was. With all of their bigness and authority, I had already figured out the truth. They did not even know who they were. How were they going to tell me who I was? No, I was the only one who could tell me who I was, and I knew I was supposed to have been born a girl.

While my heart was longing to be a girl, I was learning what it means to be a boy. The most important lessons came from my father. Every Friday of camp week there was a softball game between the boy campers and the men serving as faculty. Every single year the faculty would handily defeat the campers. Dad would spray singles past the infielders because he understood that in softball, hits were easier than home runs. The boys were all trying to prove their stuff with mighty swings that left the ball in the outfielders' mitts.

I was trying to prove my stuff, learning to row back to the dock without turning around to see where my boat was pointed. That seemed like something a twelve-year-old boy should figure out. Navigation was a man's job, or so I thought. It was Dad who drove the car, read the road maps, and knew which way to go on the trail. He was the chief navigator. Therefore, if I was going to be a man, I had better learn to navigate well, which on occasion might include moving forward while looking back.

My relationship with my parents complicated my gender identity and just about every other area of life. I loved my father and wanted to be in his presence every waking hour. He was a pastor and leader, and I viewed him as strong and invincible. If I was full of myself, it was because of the delight I brought to my father's eyes.

Dad was the youngest child of a Nickel Plate Road railcar inspector and his homemaker wife. He grew up in Martins Ferry, Ohio, a small industrial city across the Ohio River from Wheeling, West Virginia. Dad's people were Welsh and English and had come to work in the steel mills. Dad's mother had a will of steel and preordained that David Williams, the youngest of her eight children, would become a pastor. Dad never challenged his assignment or much of anything else among his mother's many expectations.

I was born three years after my father became the minister of the Westmoreland Church of Christ in Huntington, West Virginia. I came into the world at St. Mary's Medical Center, a stone's throw from the Ohio River. My mother's pregnancy had been difficult, and she was not well after I was born. For many months it was Grandma Stone who took care of me.

My relationship with my mother did not always feel safe. When I was a little older and could discern such things, I realized there was a hesitation in her parenting, as if each moment required an active decision about whether or not to engage. I was always off-balance, never knowing which mom was going to show up. Was it the fun-loving storyteller, or the depressed and fearful fundamentalist? Determining her moods became a major daily challenge.

Aware of my mother's precarious hold on her emotions, I was always searching for insight into her background. Mom was the youngest of three children of a tenant farmer in eastern Kentucky. That part of Kentucky was a Scots-Irish culture, entrenched in the paradoxical qualities of independent mindedness and clan loyalty. One of the cardinal sins was to get "too big for your britches" and climb above your family's expectations of itself. It was a world in which women married young, had children early, and did not work outside the home. It provided my mother none of the nourishment her soul desired.

As a pastor's wife, her life did not get easier. Pastors' wives were to be pretty but not too pretty, friendly, approachable, and supportive of their husbands. They were to dress nicely, but without effort and without spending money on clothes. They were to have well-behaved children who were at church with them every time the doors were open.

I understand that if I had been born a girl, my own opportunities would have been far more limited. I would not have received preferential treatment in public school or had the kinds of freedoms commonly afforded to boys in the '50s and '60s. If I had been born a girl, I would not have gotten a job as a radio announcer when I was sixteen, or received a scholarship offer in broadcasting, or been encouraged to become a public speaker.

That my mother was not able to give me the attention I needed as an infant and young child is a sad truth. A lot of cultural realities conspired to prohibit an intelligent and engaging woman from living the life she might have chosen for herself. While my mother was pre-occupied with her own struggles, Grandma Stone was a constant presence in my life. I loved spending time at her house. My grandmother's home was owned by the college in Grayson, Kentucky, where my grandfather operated the college farm. It had two small bedrooms, a living room, a kitchen, and a screened-in back porch with a summer bedroom and a summer kitchen. A summer kitchen was common in the South, where an outside stove could keep the worst of the heat out of the kitchen. I sat on Grandma's lap on the back porch as she churned butter that would soon be melting on her homemade biscuits. I spent hours with her on the front porch swing, enjoying the fragrant geraniums that covered the banister. My grandmother's house holds my earliest memories, when I knew I was loved by a woman I some-how filled with joy.

Two people I loved taught me what it meant to be a good person. My father, gentle, industrious, and devoted, was teaching me to be a gentle man. My grandmother, hardworking, affectionate, and atten-tive, was showing me that it is women who provide the nurturing that makes the world go around.

CHAPTER 3

The Problem with Puberty

We have all fought for our lives more than we know,
survived our own questions.

—ANDREA GIBSON, *THE MADNESS VASE*

When I was four, my father became the senior minister of the Noble Avenue Church of Christ in Akron, Ohio. In many ways my father's years in Akron were the highlight of his ministry career. The church was one of the largest of our denomination in Ohio, something of which I was very proud. He might be gentle and loving with me, but when Dad was out building kingdoms, he was a force. I needed him to be a force, to counteract the force at home.

Mom was struggling. She was rigid, allowing no dissent and never admitting wrongdoing. She saw her children as an extension of herself and had an ability to nullify your accomplishments by claiming them as her own. I learned to keep my good work to myself. These things I knew by the time I was an elementary school student.

Outside of my difficulties with my mother, life was good. I did well in school, had lots of friends, and was able to spend time with my father, whom I adored. During my early elementary school years, I did not struggle much with my gender. I certainly prayed often that I would wake up as a girl, and I continued to believe I should have been born a girl, but I had learned to make peace with life as a boy. It had been made clear to me that there was no other option.

During my later elementary years, my longing to be a girl increased steadily. Throughout my junior high years, it increased exponentially. I had prayed often that I would wake up as a girl, but it was more a ritual than an expectation. By seventh grade those prayers became earnest. I had the social interests and relationships expected of a boy my age, but I still felt I was supposed to have been born a girl.

I enjoyed playing with girls, as many boys do. But I also fantasized constantly about being a girl. In role-playing games with other boys, if a female role was in the script, it was mine. I especially loved playing games in which I could be a girl babysitter. I loved watching my babysitters. How did they move? What were they reading? What kind of a hairstyle did they have, and what kind of clothing was in style? I longed to be a girl babysitter.

I had a number of rituals I practiced nightly before going to sleep. I knew they weren't exactly prayers, so I called them my "thinkins." Fourteen times I repeated, "Don't let a tornado come. Don't let there be an earthquake. Don't let there be a hurricane." Fourteen times. Never mind we lived in Akron, Ohio, where a hurricane was highly unlikely. I was praying to keep the furies away. I now understand it was a prayer common to those feeling anger they are not able to express. I was angry God was not answering my prayers to be a girl. I was angry with the religiously restrictive household over which my mother presided. My anger was projected onto the storms I so feared.

Puberty arrived late, not until the summer after the ninth grade. While all of my male friends relished their lowering voices and sexual awakening, I still had the voice and body of a child. I was not disappointed. I was not ready to become a man. When my female friends went through puberty, I was distraught. I desperately wanted my body to change in all the ways their bodies were changing. I would gaze at the mirror, hoping beyond hope that my hips would broaden and my waist would remain small. I would pull and tug at the skin around my nipples, trying to get it to pool toward the center. Unfortunately, I was so skinny I could not even grab an inch of skin to form some semblance of breasts.

I watched as my girl friends all delighted in seeing their bodies change. At least that is how I imagined it. I know that is not, in fact, how most cisgender women experience their teen years. For most of them, it is a difficult time of self-consciousness. But I did not see it that way. I imagined that my female friends stood in front of the mirror for hours and admired their changing bodies. That was my fantasy. When a girl would complain about the changes her body was experiencing, I wanted to cry out, "Then for God's sake, trade places with me!" There was never a time when I prayed more fervently for God to turn me into a girl. I would lie in bed at night, after finishing my "thinkins," and imagine disappearing from the earth. It was ironic. On one hand, I was praying for no storms. On the other, I was hoping a storm would carry me away. I did not want to become a man. I wanted to become a woman.

A few months after turning fifteen, my body began to change. First, my voice became froggy and crackly and started its downward spiral. I grew much taller. My nose became far too big, and my ears stuck out. I went back to church camp at Round Lake, this time as a camper. There was a girl there, also a pastor's daughter, who I wanted to be more than any other girl I'd ever seen. She was tall, with wavy brown hair. Every evening she wore a dress to the vespers service. She took a liking to me, and we were inseparable. I'm sure most of the faculty thought it was a budding romance. To me, it was pure longing—not sexual longing, but identity longing. I would lie in bed in the boys' dorm, long after everyone was asleep, imagining sleeping soundly in the girls' dorm with all of the other girls. That was the vision that would finally allow me to fall into a fitful sleep.

The week after church camp, we moved across town, and I prepared to begin high school separated from all of the friends I had known since kindergarten. The difference between my junior high and high school experience is best illustrated by the differences in the two school bands. I played the flute, and in junior high there were four boys and four girls in the flute section. At my new high school there were sixteen flutists, and I was the only boy. I discovered that unfortunate reality on my first day of band camp.

The head majorette also served as first chair flute. In her dual role, she led our marching drills and section practices. She took one look at me and declared to the rest of the flutists, "Beanpole." The week of band camp went downhill from there. I was almost as skinny as my flute. It was excruciating. I was a freak—not yet a fully developed man, no longer a boy, and clearly nothing at all like the girls blossoming around me, the girls I so desperately wanted to be.

School started in September. I was in the tenth grade. The first day I wore a pair of blue corduroy pants and a yellow horizontal-striped button-down shirt, with penny loafers, the preppy uniform of the period. As I sat waiting to be assigned classes, I was fixated on the girl sitting across from me, who was wearing a blue skirt and a white blouse with a Peter Pan collar. Her blond hair was pulled back behind a wide headband. Though we were the only two people in the room, we never spoke. I spent the day trying not to be jealous of the different trajectories our lives would take before the day was over. She would head to class as a sophomore girl, and I would head to class in a body I disliked.

Throughout childhood I had occasionally worn a dress or shoes of my mother's. Now I did it every week. My parents were out of the house every Wednesday evening, so on those nights I began dressing in my mother's clothes. One night I was pretending to be the head majorette, the one who made fun of me during band camp, when I discovered that it felt good to touch myself while I was dressed. Before I knew it, I had my first sexual experience. I was terrified. I didn't know anything about erections or masturbation or ejaculations. I thought I had somehow damaged my body and I spent the rest of the night praying for forgiveness. For the next week I spent hours in prayer, asking God to forgive me for hurting my body. Then the next Wednesday night, I did it again.

A lot of transgender women go through a phase in which they believe they are sexual cross-dressers. It is almost inevitable. You spend years longing to be a girl, and suddenly, while you are acting out your identity, your body becomes aroused. It is confusing but exciting. It is also shame producing. It felt to me like testosterone, the effects of which I hated, had hijacked my gender identity. Why was I becoming sexually aroused by dressing as a girl? The shame was overwhelming. I did not ask for any of this. I did not ask to be transgender, and I certainly did not ask for testosterone to cause me to become aroused when I was wearing women's clothes.

Having my sexuality become entangled with my gender identity was a monumental problem that took a long time to untangle. That is not an uncommon experience for transgender women, particularly in that time period, when very little was known about gender identity and nothing was said about the differences between being transgender, a drag queen, or a sexual cross-dresser. It made what was already a difficult season even worse.

In January 1967 my father accepted a ministry with a church in Grayson, Kentucky. I was thrilled. I disliked my school in Ohio and I had always loved being with my cousins in my mother's hometown. I arrived in Kentucky with a new sense of hope.

I immediately felt comfortable at my new high school. I loved my classes and within days I had developed lasting friendships. Throughout the tumult of the previous semester, the changes to my body were rapid and significant. I grew to be over six feet tall and no longer looked like a little boy. I arrived in Kentucky a young man, and I was beginning to want to date. There was absolutely no doubt I was attracted to girls, and as soon as I got to Kentucky, there was one girl who caught my eye. She was already dating another boy, but I found the confidence to ask her out anyway. She said yes. We double-dated with my brother and his girlfriend and went to dinner and a movie in Ashland, the larger town thirty minutes away. When we sat down in the theater, I noticed her legs were only shaved to about two inches above the knee. Later on, I would discover the reason.

When I got home after the date, I realized I had quite the conundrum. My male body, now awakened by testosterone, had all the desires of a typical teenage boy. I was sexually attracted to the girl I had taken to the movies, but I also wanted to be her. I wanted to be a girl dating a girl. Over the next few months we talked a lot by phone. It was not unusual for her to start a conversation by lamenting being a girl. She told me she had always wanted to be a boy, hence the refusal to shave her legs any higher than was absolutely necessary. I came close to telling her about my own feelings. When she would talk about not being the gender she preferred, I would answer, "I know how you feel." She never took the bait and asked, "What do you mean? How could you know how I feel?" That is as close as I ever got to revealing my true self.

In the paradox that was my life, while I was longing to be a girl dating a girl, I was also being encouraged as an up-and-coming young man of promise. Opportunities started coming my way. One of my best friends was a disc jockey at the commercial radio station in town. I hung out at the station and, in the summer between my sophomore and junior years, began studying to get my Third-Class Radiotelephone Operator's License with Broadcast Endorsement, a necessity to become a radio announcer back in those days. I passed the test and the very next day started my job as a disc jockey at WGOH radio in Grayson, Kentucky. I still remember my license number: P3-19-25045.

I know why I still remember the license number. I was proud to be excelling as a teenage boy, getting the kind of job most boys would covet. It did not even occur to me that there were no girl disc jockeys. I was fully accepting of my male entitlement and proud of the standing it provided. My FCC license was a sign I had entered the club of accomplished men. At the radio station, I was interacting daily with men three times my age, yet they were treating me as their equal. It was the first time I had entered the world of men, and I was having no problem making my way.

CHAPTER 4

Escaping the Fires of Hell

Faith is a coat against . . . nakedness.

—JAMES W. FOWLER

I was in English class at Prichard High School in Grayson when I stumbled across a magazine one of my classmates brought to school. *True Story* told titillating narratives about people living on the fringes, including one story about a man who was working as a female fashion model on the runways of New York City. I read the story during a lunch break, and when everyone returned to class, I was sure every person in the building could see a scarlet *T* on my forehead. The word *transgender* was not then in existence, but *transsexual* was. I was terrified I would be discovered, but I was also desperate to learn about the condition that had accompanied me since my earliest memories.

I had read about Christine Jorgensen, the WWII American GI who went to Denmark and underwent gender confirmation surgery. I saw in *TV Guide* that she was going to be interviewed by Merv Griffin on his afternoon television show. I rushed home from school, hoping beyond hope that no one would be at the house. It was my lucky day, and I sat on the edge of the couch as the band played "I Enjoy Being a Girl." Christine Jorgensen came onstage to tell her story. She looked beautiful and happy, and I thought, *Oh my goodness! It is actually possible to transition genders. It is possible to become a woman! I could become a woman.* I was elated and terrified. It was much easier to deny my longings if it was impossible for them to be fulfilled. But now I knew the truth. It was possible to become who I truly was—a woman.

The possibility of being me had been awakened, but in the culture in which I lived, there was no way I could seriously think about acting on it. In that Scots-Irish culture, you did not stray from your roots. On my mother's side, every man was an ordained pastor, and five of my seven cousins, all women, all married pastors. My brother had become a pastor. I would go to Bible college and enter some form of ministry. I would be a man, and I would be a pastor. That was the narrative that had been laid out for me.

What I really wanted to do was transition genders and go to my freshman year of college at a state university as a girl. I would take the scholarship in broadcasting that had been offered during my senior year of high school after I received the top score at a regional speech contest. I would live in the girls' dorm with all the other coeds and learn how to be a woman. I would study English and history and journalism. I might even experiment and date boys as I tried to discern my sexual identity.

I would excel and people would take notice and I would become the most popular disc jockey at the university radio station. I would have my own interview show and be a play-by-play announcer of university basketball games. After graduation, I would move to Cincinnati or Louisville and become a television reporter, but I would not stay in that job for long, because it was my destiny to become a news anchor. I knew it was possible. As a child I had watched Dorothy Fuldheim deliver the news on WEWS-TV in Cleveland. I would do the same. That is what I daydreamed about as I worked at the radio station.

I loved television news. I watched *The Huntley-Brinkley Report* and thought John Chancellor hung the moon. There were only three television networks and no twenty-four-hour news cycle. Evening newscasters were gods. As a child I asked for a tape recorder for Christmas and recorded my own audio documentaries. When I got my dream job as a radio announcer at the ripe old age of sixteen, the possibilities seemed endless. I read the AP News like the professional I was, even though I was earning only $1.60 an hour. I reported on the Tet Offensive in the Vietnam War and rattled off the names of Vietnamese towns like I was a seasoned broadcaster. I saw the news come in over the Associated Press teletype machine that Martin Luther King Jr. had been assassinated, and I was there again when the bulletin came through that Bobby Kennedy had died.

I wanted to be a girl and I wanted to be a news anchor. Was that too much to ask? As a matter of fact, it was. Every one of my vocational dreams was the dream of an entitled White boy. With a few notable exceptions, women were not rewarded with jobs as television reporters, let alone news anchors. At the time, there were no women serving as sports color announcers, and no one would dream of allowing a woman to be a play-by-play announcer. Mine were a boy's dreams, as unrealistic for a girl as it was unrealistic for me to think I could transition genders at the tender age of eighteen.

The truth was very different from my fantasy. The path laid out for me may as well have had a WILLIAMS & SONS sign above the door. My brother and I were both expected to go to Bible college and become pastors. Much to the chagrin of my young high school teachers who wanted me to break away from religious fundamentalism, I followed my brother to Bible college. My family was very attached to the Bible college in town. My uncle was the president. My father was on the board of directors, and it had always been assumed I would attend Kentucky Christian University. By going to Bible college, I was guaranteeing a life of cognitive dissonance. My intellect would bristle, but at least for a season, my desire to transition genders might remain in check.

At a Bible college you can be expelled for drinking alcohol, smoking marijuana, having sex before marriage, or "rejecting the faith once delivered to the saints," a slippery phrase that could mean whatever the administration wanted it to mean. I attended a Bible college because it was familiar and free. But it was also a place in which I hoped I could keep my gender issues under control. Going to a Bible college would save me from eternal damnation. At least that is what I hoped.

Bible college is kind of like being at your aunt's house. You're not home, but you may as well be. Adults who look a lot like your parents have rules a lot like the ones at home. When it comes to one's social life, a Bible college is designed with one thing in mind—preventing girls from getting pregnant. When I was there, the girls had to be in their dorms by 7:30 in the evening. And what was the curfew for the guys? I'm embarrassed to say we had none. We went to the truck stop at 2:00 in the morning for a burger and fries and then rolled out of bed at 7:25 a.m. with red eyes, disheveled hair, and a can of Mountain Dew to keep us awake through 7:30 Greek class. The administrators saw no double standard. If the girls were safely in their dormitories, the school was safekeeping their virginity and their parents would be happy. It was assumed that if the girls were locked up, the boys couldn't get into too much trouble.

Our Bible college had a prayer room, the downfall of many a chaste Bible college couple. The prayer room was a sacrosanct place, with a red light outside the door to indicate someone was inside praying. Bible college culture was so insular, no one found any irony in the notion of a lit red light above a door. Apparently, we were a very spiritual school because we had a very busy prayer room.

The prayer room was little more than a large closet on an upper floor of the administration building, far enough from the hustle and bustle to be able to hear oneself think and contemplate and meditate and grope. The main social activity on our campus was walking "the circle," a stretch of asphalt between the girls' dorm, the administration building, and a quiet side street. Couples would walk in a mind-numbing circle, discussing their need for forgiveness for what they had done in the prayer room.

During my Bible college years, I gravitated toward the questioning students. One of my skeptical friends kept putting an empty Pepsi bottle outside on a window ledge and praying that God would fill it with water. God never understood the urgency of my friend's prayers and the bottle remained empty. I was never surprised when God did not show up. If there was a God and that God was inclined to answer prayer, God would certainly not make it obvious. That would be in poor form. But Bible college students were not into subtlety. They wanted certainty, like Danny, a classmate who told us about a world-class sinner he knew who on his deathbed cried out, "The devil is coming after me with hot chains!" I asked if anyone else had heard the dying man's words. Danny was evasive.

My reputation for skepticism preceded me. When you've spent your entire life praying for change and you're still transgender, you tend to be skeptical about God's inclination to answer prayer. Even though I was a Bible college student, I was already on the road of curiosity, searching for truth wherever I found it. At a Bible college, the road of curiosity was a road less traveled by. I did not find many fellow sojourners there. Most of the students were obedient rule followers, rarely coloring outside the lines.

At our Bible college, we knew nothing about homosexuality or transgenderism. Based on the occasional lectures from the dean of men, we were to assume all humans were heterosexual, sex was only for marriage, and masturbation was a sin. At my Bible college, there were no courses on human sexuality, let alone instruction on what it means to be gay or transgender. If you happened to be an LGBTQ+ student, you were out of luck. There would be no help for you. After my transition I heard from several classmates who came out after graduation. They told me about other classmates and faculty who were also gay, some of whom continue in evangelical ministries. They all described having felt great levels of guilt and shame when they were in Bible college.

None of us got the tiniest bit of help with our sexuality. You would think we might have talked about human sexuality in biology or psychology classes, but no. At my Bible college there was one biology class, and no sociology or anthropology courses. The one psychology class was a freshman course taught by the boys' basketball coach. His qualifications consisted of a bachelor's degree from our institution, which meant he had taken exactly one psychology course, probably also taught by a professor who had taken one psychology course, and so on. This is how ignorance gains momentum.

I did find one apparently caring professor, intelligent and thoughtful, who seemed like he might be a safe place to share my "problem." On several occasions I came close to telling him I was struggling with my gender identity. All I could admit, however, was that I masturbated. He asked how often. I lied and told him not very often, and he offered to check my genitalia to make sure I was not harming myself. Yes, he really did that! I was so naive I pulled down my pants and let him look. He assured me that everything looked fine and I should not worry. It felt strange, but I was so firmly entrenched in the fundamentalist bubble that I had no idea that what he was doing was abusive. Years later I found out he had done similar "examinations" on a lot of the guys on campus. I would like to think episodes like that were rare at Bible colleges. As a pastoral counselor, I know they were not. They were, in fact, quite common.

While I navigated a lot of negative realities in my four years at Kentucky Christian University, it was also a time of growth. I gained confidence as a man and as a leader. Shortly after starting college, I helped form a male quartet that traveled around the Midwest singing in churches and at conferences. We even made two albums. I cultivated a taste for Southern gospel music, and because of my job as a disc jockey, I got to spend time with famous quartets like the Oak Ridge Boys. Taking a lead role with our own quartet allowed me to flex my leadership muscles.

In my junior year, I gave my first public speech at a chapel service. My fellow students applauded, which was rare at a chapel service. The more progressive professors privately encouraged me to go on to seminary. They told me I was a good speaker with a good mind. I should be in an environment in which my mind would be challenged. While I did not immediately take their advice, I was buoyed by their encouragement.

While I was firmly within the evangelical camp, I felt no call to be a local church pastor. I did, however, want to start my postcollege years in some form of ministry. During the last half of my senior year, I recruited the best musicians I could find and invited them to move with me to Upstate New York, where they would attend another Bible college, and we would travel the eastern half of the nation singing, making albums, and putting our new quartet on the map. In December 1973 I was ordained into the Christian ministry, as my father and brother before me, and in January 1974, Cathy and I moved to Buffalo, New York.

CHAPTER 5

Till Death Do Us Part

Love is a two-way street constantly under construction.

—CARROLL BRYANT

As soon as I entered college I began searching for a wife. As an evangelical, that was the map I had been given. There would be no sex before marriage, so you looked for a wife and married young. I had dated steadily since college began, but I had not yet found the right girl.

All of that changed later in my freshman year, when our concert choir traveled to Western Pennsylvania on its spring tour. Cathy's family had driven eight hours so her older sister could spend time with another member of the choir, a student she eventually married. Cathy had caught my eye weeks earlier when her family visited our campus. She and her three sisters sang during a college chapel service, and their tight harmonies were beautiful. I have always loved tight vocal harmonies. Cathy was a petite blond with hazel eyes and a gentle countenance. I was immediately captured by her beauty. And her voice. Oh my goodness, her voice! She sang with a pure high soprano that can still bring me to tears. The voice, the eyes, the face. Her very presence demanded my attention.

Cathy and her sisters were traveling with their father, who preached for the chapel service at which they sang. The whole family came to our choir rehearsal immediately after the service, and I saw her father whisper to Cathy as I stepped out of the bass section and picked up my flute to accompany the choir on Bach's "Jesu, Joy of Man's Desiring." I wondered if he was saying something about me. Part of me hoped he was and part of me was afraid he was. He might have been saying, "My goodness, that guy is six two and a hundred and forty-five pounds and he plays the flute?! Seriously?!" Or he might have been saying, "I like the looks of that multitalented musician." Or maybe he wasn't commenting about me at all. Maybe he was just saying, "After this song I need to go to the bathroom." I arbitrarily decided he was talking about me, and what he was saying was good. It was months before Cathy told me what her father told her that day. He said, "I like that guy." My foot was in the door, and I didn't even know it.

It is fascinating how these moments of synchronicity come into our lives. I step out of the choir and pick up my flute, and the whole world changes. Time stops and the gods say, "These two precious souls shall connect and have children, and those children shall have children, and the world shall be forever changed in ways no one can fathom." That is what happened that February day in 1970. We both knew it and know it still. One moment, locked in time.

I knew I was likely to see Cathy again when the choir traveled to

Western Pennsylvania on its tour. Maybe I would be introduced to her then. When we arrived for our Pennsylvania concert, I lingered around the church reception hall, hoping to find Cathy. I did not see her until the concert began. She was sitting with her family, toward the front, house left. I began looking for her again after the concert, but before I found her, she found me. Cathy had been as eager to meet me as I had been to meet her.

As we talked that night in Somerset, Pennsylvania, Cathy was quiet and soft-spoken and so very beautiful. I saw her heart and soul, her restlessness and longing, her fierce devotion. I *saw* her, and I see her still. Cathy complimented me on the way I had accompanied the choir on the flute. I was happy to have redeemed myself. I had not played all that well the day she attended our rehearsal. I had been too nervous to maintain the embouchure the flute demands. We were in the middle of tour now, and creating the right tone was not a problem.

As we talked in a hallway of the church, I was holding a scrap of paper with the number fifteen on it. It had something to do with a mixer that was to take place later in the evening. After our long conversation, I never made it to the mixer and for some inexplicable reason, I gave the paper to Cathy, saying, "I don't need this number, because that's not something I'm going to be doing this evening."

It was about a year before Cathy told me what her thought had been on the day we first saw each other on campus. Right before her father said, "I like that guy," she saw me and thought to herself, *I'm going to marry that guy, so I'd better find out his name and meet him.* She was frightened by the unexpected thought but certain of its truth. She asked my name and hoped someone would introduce us, though it didn't happen that day. We both arrived at the Western Pennsylvania church knowing we wanted to meet each other. When I gave her the piece of paper with the number fifteen on it, she kept the paper and put it in her scrapbook, where it remains to this day. Cathy kept the paper because she thought, *I'd better keep a reminder of the person I am going to marry.*

After the concert, I stayed with the widow of a former pastor of the church. She had a stately old home, warm and welcoming. It was a cool March evening in the Western Pennsylvania highlands, and I opened the window to let in the crisp air. Lying in bed, I turned toward the window, and watching the moon rise in the night sky, I felt joy. This—this was the kind of girl I could marry! Yes. Definitely. I fell into a deep sleep.

The next day we traveled to a church in Ohio, and I began penning my first letter to Cathy, a letter I sent as soon as the tour was over. For ten days I waited anxiously to hear back from her. When I saw an envelope with beautiful handwriting in my mailbox, I knew it had to be from Cathy. I rushed to my dorm room, closed the door, and read the letter again and again. It was newsy and not at all romantic, but it was enough for me. I wrote back immediately. A few weeks later, I got up the nerve to call. Cathy's voice was as soft and expressive as I remembered. We talked about our love of music, and particularly our love of harmony. She said she was not very good at hearing harmonies, a lie born of genuine unknowing. By the time we began singing together a couple of years later, I realized she heard harmonies just fine. In fact, we both did and still do. It was part of what made us good together.

Four months after our first meeting, I was going to be attending the national convention of our denomination. When Cathy found out I was going, she told her father and he decided to bring her along. We met on the first afternoon of the convention and spent the rest of the day together. About a half hour before we would have to say good night, I reached over and took her hand. We were on the sidewalk outside Kiel Auditorium in St. Louis. Almost immediately she removed her hand from my grasp, wiped both hands together, and said, "It's hot out here." It was indeed hot and humid. I mean, after all, it was St. Louis in July. What did she expect, Chicago in winter? I was half-embarrassed and half-angry and 100 percent disappointed, but I was not giving up.

We spent the rest of the week together, but I did not try to hold her hand again until the final day. Since she had rejected my small show of affection earlier in the week, I thought a lot about what I was going to do. We would be inside, not outside. There would be no humidity, no heat, no sweat. I would reach over and gently place my hand over hers, then lock my fingers in hers ever so lightly.

We were riding the elevator to the top of the Gateway Arch when I carried out my plan. When I took her hand, I was surprised: She did not take my hand lightly. She held it firmly, and I thought, *Oh yeah. This—this is the kind of girl I could marry.*

We did not kiss until she came to our campus later that fall. Cathy and her sisters sang for a banquet at the school, and afterward, we sat on the front porch of my cousin's house, right on the edge of campus. Cathy was in a light-pink dress. Her hands were on her lap and I again took one of them. She again held my hand tightly. I let go of her hand and put my arm lightly around her shoulders. Then I turned her head toward mine. I looked in her eyes and kissed her. It was only a whisper of a kiss, but it was electric, the feel of her soft lips against mine. I touched the bare skin of her neck as I kissed her lightly again. That was it—two soft kisses. With those two whisper kisses, I knew this was not just the *kind* of girl I could marry. This was *the* girl I wanted to marry.

The next morning, Cathy left for New York. I was lovesick. I wrote her that day, and twice a week until Christmas. Over the holidays our quartet traveled to New York to present concerts at churches in the region. I stayed at her house. From the time I arrived, we were inseparable. Cathy's parents were keeping a close watch over us, so over the first few days we did not get much time alone. When we finally did find a chance for solitude, we went downstairs and sat together in a large easy chair in her family room. The radio was playing a middle-of-the-road FM station, the kind of music I played every night in my job as a disc jockey. B. J. Thomas's tune "Raindrops Keep Fallin' on My Head" was playing when I put my arm around Cathy and pulled her close. Then I kissed her—not a whisper kiss, but a proper kiss, long and full. We kissed for hours, so long and intensely that we both had swollen lips the next morning. I don't mean slightly swollen. I mean bee-stung lips, the kind that caused everyone to look and quickly glance away, as if they had seen a vision not intended for the public.

Our quartet left a few days later, but before we piled into the station wagon, I asked Cathy to go steady and she said yes. We exchanged class rings. She wrapped my white gold ring in blue yarn so it would fit her finger, and I wore her yellow gold ring on the little finger of my left hand. I returned to Kentucky knowing I had been with the girl I wanted to marry. I was nineteen and Cathy was seventeen.

That August her older sister was married in New York. I sang at the wedding. Cathy was the maid of honor. When I saw her on the day of the wedding, I was overwhelmed with desire. I can still remember her coming down the aisle. Having just sung, I was in the front row by the organ and had an unobstructed view as she slowly made her way to the front. Throughout the wedding I could barely take my eyes off of her.

When the reception was over, Cathy's father asked if we wanted to drive the bride and groom to the Statler Hilton Hotel in Manhattan, where they were going to honeymoon. As we drove back to Long Island with all the streamers still on the car, people honked and waved, thinking it was our honeymoon. I was thrilled. I knew I wanted to marry Cathy. Right after the ceremony ended, before the reception line formed, I took Cathy aside and whispered in her ear, "You could not have been any more beautiful in the mind of God when he first thought of you than you are today." The next afternoon she handed me a piece of stationery and asked me to write down what I had told her the day before. I wrote the words in my best handwriting and she kept the note. It is still in her scrapbook next to the number fifteen. I drove back to Kentucky the following day. Three weeks later the fall semester began.

Cathy had decided to attend Kentucky Christian University, and the day she arrived for freshman orientation, I made sure I did not have to work at the radio station. I helped her move into her dorm room, introduced her to my friends, and saw to it that she signed up for the concert choir auditions. The director already knew about her voice. He'd heard her sing with her sisters. She was selected for the choir, and I was thrilled. We would be in rehearsal together three times a week, and on tour in the spring. I did not let Cathy out of my sight during freshman orientation or the first couple of weeks of school. I saw how the other guys were looking at her. We were inseparable through the semester, but there was one thing that was bothering me. Cathy still had not told me that she loved me.

When I began dating Cathy, I immediately recognized she was as restless a soul as I was. She was someone who would not be content until her soul found its rhythm. That is part of what drew me to her. She was also asking questions for which our church had no answers.

I liked that about her. Cathy was opinionated and thoughtful and expectant. She was complicated, and I have always been drawn to complicated. She was not an open book.

Cathy had a heart for racial and social justice. She taught Sunday school in a storefront church in a depressed part of Queens, New York, and loved working with children. From the time we first met, Cathy talked about adopting a child from a foreign country. Once we began dating seriously, she wanted to make sure I shared her desire. Though she still had not professed her love, Cathy was discerning whether or not I was the man she wanted to marry.

Cathy had been taught that telling someone you love them is as good as a declaration of intent to marry. That was why she had not yet told me she loved me. She was terrified to tell me. In her mind, that meant we would marry, and she knew she was too young to marry. The truth is that we were both too young.

One day when we were "praying" in the prayer room, my hands wandered under Cathy's blouse. It felt like heaven, but we both thought we had committed some kind of grievous sin. I felt awful. That evening we had a long conversation about our feelings for each other. We were both frustrated with the college's ridiculous rules and regulations about dating: "You can hold hands, and you can hug and kiss, but not for extended periods of time." The handbook did not define the exact nature of "extended periods of time." Conservative classmates regularly confronted Cathy in the dorm, saying, "I know what you and Paul are doing, and it is wrong. Purity is godliness." Of course, what we were doing was hugging and kissing, a lot, for extended periods of time. But in that environment, even that show of affection was to be reserved for marriage.

What happened in the prayer room felt wonderful, glorious even, just as it should have. Other than knowing we were in violation of the student handbook, we did not feel guilty, because there was nothing about which to feel guilty. I was mostly worried that Cathy felt bad about what happened. After we talked, we both fell into silence. A couple of minutes later, Cathy looked at me and said, "It's okay, Paul. I love you." Finally, she told me she loved me. We hugged and kissed, a lot, for an extended period of time.

During the next semester, Cathy and I began talking about our life goals. We both wanted to have three children. We both came from frugal homes, where you did not spend more money than you had and saved every penny you could. We both loved music and enjoyed singing. We had a hunger to know God, regardless of the direction in which that hunger took us. We seemed sexually compatible, though under the circumstances, how could we really know? As I pondered these things, I wondered if she was feeling the same way.

I was surprised when on a warm April day, while we were stepping across a stream at Carter Caves State Park in eastern Kentucky, Cathy asked, "Are we going to get married or what?" I stared at the rocks in the creek that ran beneath the natural bridge in the park. There had been little rain that winter, and pools of stagnant water were scattered here and there, waiting for the spring rains to wake them from their slumber. I stepped from rock to rock trying to figure out how to answer. I had been so busy chasing Cathy, I had not thought about what I would do if I actually caught her. Now she caught me, and I wasn't ready. I fumbled for words and didn't give a direct answer. The drive back to campus was awkward.

In bed that night I thought about the day. I was still burying my feelings that I should have been born a girl. Over the next several weeks I dreamed about wanting to be a girl, but I also dreamed about making love to Cathy. The most frightening dream was one in which I was a girl, making love to Cathy. I shoved that dream deep into my subconscious self. I was not going to let my life be ruined by being transgender. I was a man and would remain so, and I would marry the girl I loved.

A few weeks later, when I was working my evening shift at the radio station, I was playing the Carpenters' tune "We've Only Just Begun." As I listened to the soft harmonies and the words *white lace and promises*, I said aloud, "There comes a time when you just have to commit." That was it. I ordered our wedding rings the next morning.

The rings arrived less than three weeks later. I kept taking the engagement ring and wedding bands from their boxes and feeling the surface of the burnished yellow and white gold. I would put Cathy's engagement ring on the little finger of my left hand while putting my wedding band in its rightful place on my ring finger. It was thrilling to slip Cathy's ring on my little finger, but there was also a thrill in putting on my own ring. That was my dilemma.

I had grown accustomed to life as a man. I was a good student with great job prospects. I thought I would be a good husband and father. But I also adored that oh-so-beautiful engagement ring, with its glittering diamond. I liked my ring, but my heart skipped a beat when I put Cathy's ring on my finger. Was it skipping because of my love for Cathy, or because I was wearing the ring? Both were true. I did love Cathy, but I also loved seeing that diamond on my finger. I was no match for the magnitude of my dilemma. Burying my ambivalence, I drove to Canton, Ohio, where Cathy and her sisters were singing for a church conference.

Late on the evening of Thursday, June 22, 1972, outside the front doors of the Ohio church, I got on my knee and asked Cathy to marry me. No one else was present. It was just the two of us. Cathy gave a little squeal and hugged me and whispered in my ear, "Yes! Yes! I will marry you." At that moment, I felt like a man—a strong, happy, expectant man. The engagement ring did not belong on my finger. It belonged on hers. I thought I could hold on to that feeling forever.

The feeling did remain for the rest of June and the first half of July. It was not until late July that I began having a sense of unease while I was mowing the cemetery. Still, in spite of my discomfort, I did not think about calling off the wedding. The late summer and fall were busy preparing for the ceremony: choosing invitations, bridesmaids' dresses, color schemes, and music, and writing vows. I was more involved than most guys I knew, but I did not think it was highly unusual. I was just enjoying the details of our coming nuptials. I began working overtime shifts at the radio station to save money for our honeymoon. We would start on Long Island, go to a cabin in the Pocono Mountains of Eastern Pennsylvania, then head back to Kentucky.

The Christmas season arrived with a flurry of activity. Final exams were particularly taxing, since I was taking one of the most difficult courses in the history program at the college, a class in the history of our denomination, which is known as the Stone-Campbell Movement. The denomination had two branches: the Stone branch from Kentucky and the Campbell branch from Western Pennsylvania, each named after their respective leaders. My family's involvement with the denomination went back five generations on the Kentucky side and three on the Ohio side. I wanted to do well in the course. I aced the final, getting 100 percent for the entire semester. For all of my doubts about the church, my roots ran deep in the Stone-Campbell Movement. It was my heritage, and I looked forward to bringing another generation into its familiar embrace.

Final exams and Christmas concerts over, we loaded up our 1971 Chevrolet Nova and drove to New York. My brother and other groomsmen would fly in for the wedding. My parents and two of my cousins would drive. They would all arrive just two days before the wedding on December 31, 1972.

Other than taking place during a driving rain, our wedding day was wonderful. The ceremony itself was lovely, even though it was obvious we had not thought through Cathy's father's suggestion that we have the wedding just before midnight on New Year's Eve. By the time we left the church, we were exhausted.

I was extremely distraught when I awoke the morning after the wedding and stared at the Holiday Inn ceiling, whispering to myself, "Oh God, I'm in the wrong body." I thought those feelings had been locked away where they would never see the light of day. I had been ignoring the promptings of my soul since childhood and had kept them buried since the previous summer. I was still acting as if my gender issues were going to be miraculously cured with marriage. But now I was married, and they were not cured. While sex was wonderful, when I woke up that morning, I knew getting married was not going to wash away the fact that I was supposed to have been born a girl.

My testosterone-pumped body clearly wanted male sex, but my soul wanted something else. I found it frustrating that my male body focused so much on the act itself, as if it had its own agenda: leaving seed, creating offspring, and doing it all over again. It felt foreign and somehow wrong. I wanted to be with a woman. Of that I had no doubt. I wanted to be with Cathy, whose soul was as precious as her body. But my body and spirit were not aligned. My body was getting in the way of making love, and the sense of disconnection was shame producing. I thought of what the French call the moment of orgasm—*la petite mort*, the little death. My body longed for a different kind of feeling. I wanted our two bodies to be similar.

On New Year's night we made love again, late into the evening. I was already burying my feelings from early that morning. It was a satisfying night. Denial can be good, protecting us from the truths we do not yet have the resources to accept. The next morning, we left for the Pocono Mountains. I have only pleasant memories of the rest of our honeymoon and the first few weeks we were in our new home on campus. We were married, and we were looking forward to a long future together.

CHAPTER 6

Life Together

*You don't choose your family. They are God's gift to you,
as you are to them.*

—DESMOND TUTU

During my last semester of college, I decided on a rather unorthodox career choice. I would start my own vocal band. I had fallen in love with Southern gospel music during my high school years and thoroughly enjoyed singing with a quartet during my college years. I knew making a living with my own band would be difficult, but after long conversations with Cathy, I decided to pursue work with a national youth organization as their Northeast director. Our vocal band would travel the Northeast, working with churches and youth programs.

I wanted to be a successful provider, a good husband, a caring father, and a good Christian man. All of my goals were in alignment with my evangelical upbringing. Going any deeper was fraught with peril because every time I did listen to my heart, I still struggled with the consistent feeling I should have been born a girl.

I had never told Cathy I was transgender. Since the subject had been so much on the back burner during my college years, I was confident it was going to go away once I got married. When that didn't happen, I did not know what to do. It would have been better to have told Cathy before we married, and I regretted not having done so. Even now that we were married, I was not sure I could tell her the whole truth—that I wished I had been born a girl. I could hardly tell myself the whole truth.

I chose an evening when I would not be traveling the next weekend. We sat down in the living room, and I told Cathy that what I was going to say was big, but I did not think it was an insurmountable problem. I said that from the time I was a small child, I had found comfort dressing as a girl. I had done it since I was three or four years old, and afterward it always filled me with great shame. I told her that during my college years I thought it had gone away, but now it had returned.

Cathy listened intently, and when I finished, she said, "I love you, Paul. This does not change my love for you." We both cried and hugged and talked quite a while before going to bed relieved. We would solve my problem together. Unfortunately, that is what we called it—"my problem." Identifying my gender dysphoria as "my problem" only served to increase my shame.

Cathy and I were both naive. We had no idea our optimism was based on nothing more than wishful thinking. The truth is I am glad we did not know the full measure of what was to come. We weren't ready for it. Our priority was having children and raising a family. Had we known earlier, would we have had children? Would we have stayed together? It is impossible to know. At the time, very little was known about gender dysphoria. I had found one single book that had any information at all, and it had exactly two pages about the subject. Those two pages were hopeful. They said it was a "complex and perplexing ailment that could be worked through with great effort." The book did not suggest how this could be done, but I found comfort in that one sentence.

Had I told Cathy the entire truth, that I wished I had been born a girl, we could have grown together in our understanding and discovered what it might mean for our relationship going forward. But it was too frightening to face the full truth. There is so much that was unfair to Cathy. It is hard to make peace with it all. I was convinced I could "work through" the issue, though I didn't know exactly how. I was terrified of losing my livelihood and my marriage. We were young, too young. I was twenty-two and Cathy was twenty. It is difficult to extend grace to my twenty-two-year-old self, but there is no other way to make peace with the past and move on.

A transgender woman lived down the road from us. A neighbor who worked at the corner store said, "I hate when he [misgendering the woman] is a customer. It is disgusting, a man in a dress." Her words stung. If it ever became known I was anything like that woman, my career would be over. I told Cathy how important it was that she told no one what I had told her. For another nine years she did not have a single person with whom she could talk about what I had revealed to her. It was 1983 before we both entered therapy and had someone with whom we could speak. Until then, it was just the two of us.

The next couple of years were busy as I worked with our quartet and a youth organization. Cathy and I both volunteered with the church youth program. Three years after we married, we decided to have children.

We found out we were going to become parents a few months before our nation's bicentennial celebration. Cathy's pregnancy went smoothly, and Jonathan was born in January 1977, four weeks before one of the biggest snowstorms in the history of Western New York. I took comfort in the fact that while she was pregnant, I had no desire to be pregnant. Cathy's pregnancy was hers, and I was pleased, even thrilled, to be a father. The moment I saw Jonathan, I knew I was going to be happy as a dad. I was not going to allow my gender identity to interfere with being the best father I could be. To this day I would not trade the experience of fatherhood for anything. The years my children were at home were the most peaceful of my life.

Three years after Jonathan was born, we began the process of adopting our daughter, Jael. We settled on a program in Kolkata, India, and began the laborious work of applications, home study investigations, immigration approvals, and everything else necessary to complete an international adoption. I took charge of the process and worked diligently to bring Jael home. One might think that for a transgender woman, such an experience might feel somewhat akin to birthing my daughter, but it did not feel that way at all. I was just a father laboring to bring his daughter home.

After suffering from failure to thrive, Jael was finally able to travel to New York when she was two months old. The orphanage director said, "I'm not sure she will survive in the United States, but I know she won't survive here." We took Jael to the doctor every day and her physicians became close friends. Neither was confident she would live through those early months, but against all odds, Jael thrived. She had a fight in her eyes that told us she was going to be fine.

Jana came into the world just thirteen months after Jael's arrival.

She brought a calm joy to both Cathy and me, and we loved having a son and two daughters. Our dream of having three children had become a reality.

As is typical in most families, Cathy carried the bulk of the parenting responsibilities. Men think they are doing an equal amount of parenting, but most of the time they are not. Since transitioning, I cannot count the number of times I have said to Cathy, "I am so sorry. I just never understood." When I was a man, I certainly did not realize how many more hours a week a woman works than a man. I get it now. Women have two full-time jobs: one at work and one at home. Men have a full-time job at work and a part-time job at home. They just think the job at home is full-time. It is the mothers who are truly working two full-time jobs.

There are so many ways in which a man does not understand the world in which a woman lives. I now realize why it takes so long for a woman to get ready to leave the house. First, she is the one who has to get the children ready. She picks out their clothes and has to say, "No, you are not wearing a bathing suit and tights; it's December!" Then, with the child thrashing about on the floor, it is the mother who has to argue with the intransigent child while the father impatiently rattles his keys. After that has happened for each of the three children, the mother can finally get herself ready to go.

I still do not have to worry about getting children ready, and grandchildren are just enough out of their element to avoid scenes of thrashing about in bathing suits and tights. But as a woman, it is plenty time-consuming just getting myself ready.

I get a haircut half as often as I used to, but it costs ten times as much. Ten times as much! It is my hair, which I understand causes hairdressers sleepless nights. But still, ten times as much? I also have to get my hair colored every five weeks, which itself costs about as much as a good used car. I mean, I could let my hair go gray, but that's not about to happen.

Here is a sentence you will never hear spoken to a man: "That's not a great haircut for a man over fifty." You won't hear that because America doesn't care if a man looks like he's over fifty—or sixty or seventy, for that matter. Women ask, "Who is your hairstylist?" as if to say, "Do you even have a hairstylist? And if you do, does she know you're over fifty?"

I also understand why women need a larger wardrobe than men. You can't wear khakis and a blue sport coat every time you leave the house, like I did when I was a guy. People remember if you've worn that fuchsia jacket before and they judge you for it. Well, women judge you. Men have no idea if you've worn the fuchsia jacket before because, well, they're men.

Jeans and button-down shirts and sport coats and khakis are all I owned as a guy. I shopped in two places: Brooks Brothers and Bills. Bills khakis are indestructible. They will outlast civilization. If you are a man of a certain age and standing, you can wear Bills and Brooks Brothers anywhere. You'll be a little underdressed for Wall Street, but you'll get along just fine on Main Street. You can even buy Brooks Brothers stuff at the airport. There are only about ten styles in the small airport store, but that's all you need. A solid button-down shirt, a gingham-check button-down, and you're done.

As a woman, I do most of my shopping online because I am one of the few women who can. I can buy a pair of size ten tall jeans from any online retailer in America, and they will fit perfectly. There is something suspicious about that. Cathy can go into a department store and try on twenty pairs of jeans and none will fit. Yet I can buy jeans from any online retailer. How can that be?

Clothing companies make jeans for tall, skinny women with no curves, a body type that does not reflect 99 percent of the female pop-ulation. Or let's be really honest—they make women's jeans for tall, skinny men, not cisgender women. That is because they make clothes for models, not most of the women I know, and female models are shaped like tall, skinny boys—hence, my ease buying jeans.

I buy a lot of my clothes from Old Navy because their tall clothing fits and it's inexpensive. A woman does not have three pairs of jeans, like a guy. She has fifteen, because they are all tight and if you gain two pounds, you can't wear eight of them. And again, you can't wear the same pair over and over because people will talk. If you are going to wear a pair of jeans only once every three weeks, they do not have to be Brooks Brothers quality. Old Navy will do. The jeans might fall apart after six months, but that's okay because the style will have changed by then anyway.

Sweaters are tricky because all women's sweaters have armholes designed for stick figures. If you have average-size female upper arms, sweaters make you look like a male bodybuilder. Women's sweaters also start balling up after you wear them twice. That is because the quality of women's clothing is about half the quality of men's cloth-ing. If I bring a sweater home from the store, it's typically lost a but-ton before I wear it the first time. It is also why they have to give you an extra button with every sweater. I am also assuming the lack of quality is why it costs twice as much to dry-clean women's clothing. I'm guessing women's clothes fall apart in the dry-cleaning machine.

I do not wear dresses very often. I thought I would, but I wear them only occasionally. It turns out that after you transition, you do not do a lot of things you thought you would when you became a woman. I thought I would wear dresses and never wear sweats. Now I wear sweats and rarely wear dresses. I also do not wear heels. I have one pair and they are on a top shelf, covered in dust. Part of the reason is because I am over six feet tall, and heels are just plain uncomfortable, an invention designed to bedevil the days of women.

I do have a closet full of shoes, because my pink-white-yellow-and-green-polka-dot Tieks ballet flats cannot be worn every day. They are not the Mephisto loafers I used to wear everywhere except to a formal dinner. The polka-dot Tieks go with exactly four outfits. I have many pairs of Tieks. They are expensive but comfortable. Finding comfortable shoes is now a quest. My quest used to be climbing fourteen-thousand-foot mountains. Now it's finding good shoes.

I spend half of my budget on makeup. I have a love-hate relationship with Sephora. All other makeup causes my face to break out like a fourteen-year-old, but everything at Sephora is so expensive it requires an installment loan. My mascara costs thirty-four dollars, and my foundation thirty-eight dollars. But Sephora does have perks, like their VIP points, which are worth free samples of things you would never actually use in real life.

I now know why women carry large purses. First, it is because you were hurrying so much to leave the house that you forgot to put on hand cream or lipstick, so you'd better have a backup supply. You also carry a large purse because the world needs you to carry a large purse. People need snacks, tissues, Band-Aids, hair ties, ibuprofen, chewing gum, breath mints, and all manner of necessities. They look to you for these things. Your purse needs to be as large as a corner bodega.

Since transitioning, I cannot count the number of times I have said to Cathy, "Oh, I am so, so sorry. I just didn't know." It can't be easy for her. Occasionally she does say, "Oh, I tried to tell you. Trust me—I tried." But she never lashes out. She's just glad I finally understand. Better late than never, I suppose.

I speak often on the differences between life as a woman and life as a man. While I am beginning to understand just how much of the parenting responsibility falls to mothers, and that our family was no exception, I also am reminded just how much I loved being a father.

Jonathan was born in Williamsville, New York, and we continued to live in Western New York for the first two and a half years of his life. We started the process of adopting Jael while there, but finished the adoption on Long Island, where I took a job as a fundraiser for the ministry with which I worked for the next thirty-five years. The organization started new churches in the New York City area. While Cathy was caring for our children, I was raising money and traveling around the country speaking at conferences and churches. I finished my first master's program and a few years later my second, both focused on ministry.

After ten years raising funds and helping start new churches, I became the CEO of the ministry and stayed in that role for the next twenty-two years. The entrepreneurial nature of the work appealed to me. I wanted work that required me to start something from scratch and recruit others to buy into my vision. I went into the field of church planting because it was entrepreneurial work, and I was definitely an entrepreneur.

The term *church planting* was coined by evangelical seminaries in the 1980s as courses on starting churches became popular. I was one of the early members of our denomination to earn a master's degree in the subject, and when I became the third director in the history of the ministry, I decided to use my knowledge to help start new churches that would grow more rapidly than the churches we had planted in the past. I also wanted to start churches that embraced intellectual curiosity, encouraged honest inquiry, and appealed to those who had been wounded by traditional evangelical Christianity.

To a small degree, that is what we built at the Orchard Group, the new name we gave the ministry. We started churches that appealed to the unchurched and those who had not been to church since childhood. I thought we were progressive and cutting-edge, and in the realm of methodology, we were. We started churches with sophisticated hiring processes, multiple pastors, great music, and good advertising. Our church buildings looked like giant coffee shops, with polished concrete, high ceilings, and open spaces. We became successful and grew beyond our self-imposed boundaries of the metropolitan New York City area. Over the thirty-five years I was with the ministry, we grew from a budget of $167,000 to a budget of $4 million and expanded to serve the entire United States, becoming one of the largest church planting ministries in the nation.

Within the evangelical bubble, our ministry was cutting-edge, but within the larger social milieu, we were a modern-age relic, creating churches that were fortresses of traditional thinking. We were not affirming of the LGBTQ+ population and only appealed to people who held a more conventional faith, with a focus on who goes to heaven and who goes to hell. We were espousing a religion of rules and regulations.

When I attended Bible college and was ordained by a conservative denomination, I had locked myself into a career path that required fealty to evangelical theology. As I progressed in my career, I realized that was not the smartest decision I ever made. I was far too curious to tolerate evangelical narrow-mindedness. I appreciated the pragmatism and methodology of the evangelical world, but as I grew older and wiser, evangelical theology was no longer tenable to me. The evangelical world was focused on doctrine, saving people from hell, and creating churches that were places for evangelicals to circle the wagons against popular culture. My own theology was moving in the opposite direction.

I kept a lot of my shifting beliefs to myself and respectfully worked within the tradition in which I had been raised. At the same time, I was also looking for opportunities to change our ministry from within. I truly believed that an important part of spiritual health is the vigor with which you pursue the truth. While I understood that the truth can be difficult to discern, I firmly believed that if the truth can be discerned, it will set you free. That conviction charted my course and slowly, but inexorably, led me away from evangelicalism and toward a more generous expression of Christianity.

CHAPTER 7

Will This Decision Enhance
Your Life or Diminish It?

You can't go home again.

—THOMAS WOLFE

While our children were still at home, there was no way I was going to consider transitioning. It was important that they be able to navigate through their adolescence without the trauma of a parent transitioning genders. I thought my feelings might change once they were out of the house, but they did not. I knew if I transitioned, it would be hard for all three. In real and important ways, they would lose their father. The thought of my family going through that kind of pain was more than enough for me to commit to remaining a husband and father for as long as I possibly could.

I looked to psychotherapy as one of the guides to help me continue my life as Paul. In 1993 I began working with Naomi, my New York therapist. She was a wonderful psychotherapist, seasoned and competent. I believe psychotherapy is a healthy process for the majority of people, though few who begin therapy follow it through to completion. Many drop out before dealing with their deepest issues. Staying the course is hard work. Naomi was a masterful guide on a groundbreaking journey. While I was in therapy, I was also completing a doctor of ministry degree in pastoral care. The degree would enable me to become a pastoral counselor.

Most pastoral counselors utilize the same techniques used by other mental health professionals but add a spiritual element. Carl Jung defined a psychoneurosis as the soul's failure to discover its meaning. I believe my job as a pastoral counselor is to guide my clients through the laborious but rewarding process of discovering their soul's meaning. The answers lie within each client. It is my job to help them remove the obstacles that prevent them from finding those answers.

I chose to become a pastoral counselor rather than a licensed clinical counselor, as Cathy had done after serving as an elementary school teacher for fifteen years. While most of my reasons for going into ministry were tied to the expectations of my parents, once I was in ministry, I found great satisfaction helping people puzzle through life's deepest spiritual questions. "Why am I here, and for what purpose?" Those questions lie at the core of humanity's search for meaning, and becoming a pastoral counselor put me in the right spot to help people find their own answers to those important questions.

For much of my adult life, I had very few people with whom I could puzzle through such existential questions. Byron was my first mentor. Chairman of the philosophy department at an East Coast university, he was also a devoted Christian from within my own religious tradition. Jim was another mentor. The former rector of the Roman Catholic seminary on Long Island, he was also a philosopher and theologian, well acquainted with the rich spiritual tradition of the church fathers and mothers. Both men were influential in my life. I met with Byron twice a month, and we studied philosophy and theology together. Jim led a reading group I was a part of for over twenty-five years. That group was instrumental in helping me break free from evangelicalism and embrace a more generous expression of the Christian faith. It was also a major source of friendship and encouragement. Those two mentors, that reading group, a few other close friendships, and my therapist all combined to accelerate my journey forward through the desert. Now that I could see green pastures ahead, I wanted to serve as a guide for others on a similar journey.

A doctor of ministry degree is what is known as a terminal degree, the highest professional degree within the field of ministry. The degree would allow me to combine spiritual and psychological growth, disciplines to which I had devoted a great deal of personal energy. By committing to a doctor of ministry degree in pastoral care, I was also committing to undoing some of the damage that has been done by many evangelical Christian counselors.

In my experience, some of the most dangerous counselors are evangelical Christians who confront clients with the supposedly clear teachings of the Bible. "If the Bible says homosexuality and being transgender are wrong, then they are wrong." In taking such a simplistic view of scripture, Christian counselors do a great disservice to their clients. I remember a Christian counselor who complained that secular therapists "see religion as the problem." Well, sometimes religion is the problem. In fact, a lot of the time bad religion is the genesis of serious distress. But as any good pastoral counselor knows, healthy spirituality can be a solution to the damage done by bad religion.

Much of my early work with Naomi was not in the realm of spirituality. It was centered around my family of origin. We mined my childhood for one overriding reason: that was where the gold was. When narcissism is present in a family, the entire family system is affected. For those who are seen as little more than an extension of a narcissistic family member, the wounds run deep. I had always been afraid that the genesis of my gender issues might be my childhood experience with my mother. It was an area I had to explore. Naomi helped me understand just how ill my mother was, and how fortunate I had been to have a father who was able to lessen the effect of her illness. She also helped me understand that no amount of bad parenting can cause a person to be transgender.

As time went on, Naomi and I began to focus more heavily on my gender dysphoria (the technical term used in the *DSM-5*—the *Diagnostic and Statistical Manual of Mental Disorders*—to define a person dealing with gender-identity issues). It was a long slog. Did searching for its origins help? With my level of intellectual curiosity, it most certainly did. Did it change the outcome? Probably not, but I needed the long, slow process of psychodynamic therapy to chart a path forward.

I loved my work with Naomi, but by the early 2000s it was clear that while most parts of my life were coming together, my gender issues were becoming more problematic. When I first entered into therapy, I was still operating from a map that said gender dysphoria was a paraphilia that needed to be overcome. Through my work with Naomi, I realized gender dysphoria is not a paraphilia. Gender identity, like sexual identity, is at the core of one's being. To deny it is to deny yourself permission to be you.

When I came to know that profound truth, I entered a period of moderate depression. Moderate depression, like moderate turbulence when you are flying, is a lot worse than the word would indicate. I could barely get up in the morning. I would get better as the day progressed, but then I would dread going to bed at night, because I knew I would wake up the next morning depressed again. Day after day there was no relief. I was able to go to work, but my productivity plummeted. I would sit and stare for an hour before pulling myself together to do a couple of hours of work. There were few tears, but there was also little laughter and very little joy. I was just existing, with not much thought about the past and little concern for the future. It was a dark period.

I did not become depressed overnight. I had been mildly depressed since my children were in their teens. Jonathan graduated from high school in 1995, Jael in 1998, and Jana in 1999. As the new millennium arrived, Cathy had gotten a job teaching in Long Island's Bay Shore School District, and we were both working through empty-nest syndrome. Now that the children were gone, we realized just how much our relationship had been centered around parenting. I was focused on growing the Orchard Group while Cathy was engaged in a fulfilling teaching position. While our careers were progressing nicely, my gender dysphoria was not getting better, and our marriage was not getting stronger.

Jael returned home to finish college and was there to witness the worst of my depression. It was difficult for Cathy and Jael to see me so down. They did not know whether to comfort me or push me through it. With mild to moderate depression, I found it helpful to be pulled out of my isolation. My moderate depression had begun in the fall of 2003, and by the spring of 2004, I was feeling a lot better, but my depression was still there, like a dark lens that distorted my vision.

During this period, I did have two wonderful areas of reprieve from my struggle with depression and being transgender. I became the editor-at-large of the national magazine of our denomination, which had been published every week since 1866. I wrote a weekly column and helped the editor set themes and choose writers. I loved the work. The editor, Mark, was a good friend and respected colleague. We spent a lot of time crafting the theme of each issue and thinking about what the people of our denomination needed from the magazine.

From 1998 through 2011 I also served as an on-air host and head writer for the Worship Network, a nationwide television network that did the overnight programming for PAX TV. We were a low-key religious network. You could tell we were Christian, but by design you had no idea if we were conservative or liberal, Catholic or Protestant. The show, simply titled *Worship*, consisted of scenes of nature, soothing music, and a host who told a story in three parts. I served as one of the hosts and loved my work with the network. I will always be grateful for the friendships I developed there.

In 2006 we moved the main office of the Orchard Group from Long Island to Massachusetts, and later to Manhattan. I did not realize how difficult it would be to surrender the culture we had developed over two decades at our Long Island office. I loved my co-workers, and when I was no longer with them day to day, it was difficult. Both the magazine and television network were taking up some of the slack, but it was not the same. Two women in particular, Brigida and Anne, had been my closest co-workers, along with Jim, our director of non-English-speaking ministries. Now they were gone. While I remained as CEO, I was not leading the day-to-day work of the ministry. We had hired a chief operating officer who did most of the heavy lifting, and I was struggling to adjust.

In the spring of 2006, Cathy was ready for a change of scenery and said, "I'd like to take a leave of absence from my teaching position and move to Colorado for a year or two to see if we'd like living there. If I can get a teaching job, we'll have two years to decide whether or not to return." I knew as long as I had an apartment in New York, working remotely from Colorado would not be a problem. In April 2006 we traveled to Colorado so Cathy could look for a job.

Jonathan had finished college in Colorado and Jana had moved there before marriage. Jael was also in the West, working in Phoenix. For the better part of fifteen years I had spent four weeks a year hiking in the Colorado Rockies and had fallen in love with the region, so I agreed with Cathy that it might be a good place for the next chapter of our lives. Teachers were paid half as much in Colorado, but Cathy had spent her entire life in New York and was ready to move.

Cathy was able to get a teaching job in Longmont, Colorado, and in the summer of 2006, we moved to the northern suburbs of Denver. We sold our house in East Islip where we had lived for twenty-four years and moved into a rental home on Colorado's Front Range. I kept an apartment on Long Island for my monthly trips back to New York, but for the first time since 1973, my primary residence was no longer in New York State. I joined the preaching team of a megachurch in Boulder County where Rick, one of my best friends, was the lead pastor. I preached seven or eight times a year, and the church provided ample opportunities to develop friendships and acclimate to life in Colorado.

I was struggling more than ever with my gender identity. While I loved living in Colorado, I brought my tortured self with me. Shortly after settling into our rented home, Cathy said, "I don't know what is wrong with you, but I'm not sure how long I can live with this. I hope

I did not move to Colorado to get divorced." It was the first time in our lives either one of us had talked about divorce. I was terrified. I was sure I would not survive it.

I never thought my gender issues would bring about the end of our marriage. Yes, it was a problem, and yes, the more depressed I became, the more difficult it was to nurture our relationship, but in the world in which we lived, marriage was for life. Period. Until she spoke those words, I never even thought about the possibility of splitting up. I was so frightened I became sick to my stomach and had to step outside to gather my thoughts. Could we really divorce because I was transgender? Surely not.

Around the time we moved to Colorado, other stressors in our lives were diminishing. The move coincided with my stepping down from day-to-day management of the Orchard Group. My major responsibilities had shifted to oversight, fundraising, hiring and mentoring pastors, and leading church boards. During this period, I completed my doctor of ministry degree and became nonexecuive chairman of the board.

I hand-selected my replacement as CEO. Brent, my successor, had proven himself to be a hard worker and wonderful confidant in the five years he worked as our chief of operations. Our development director, David, was the third member of our senior leadership team. I loved working with both men. David was outgoing and affable, and a great encouragement to me. Brent was focused and efficient, implementing the agenda we had developed together. Two times a year we traveled to Rocky Mountain National Park to hike or snowshoe. We thoroughly enjoyed our time together as we dreamed and strategized about the future.

During this period of ministry, I was doing satisfying work. A lot of my time was spent counseling pastors, particularly pastors whose churches were growing rapidly. In addition to my work mentoring and counseling pastors, I was also helping shape the overall direction of our ministry. During my later years with the Orchard Group, I began talking with some of our pastors about my support of the LGBTQ+ population. I had come to a supportive theological position in the 1980s but had not spoken about it within my denomination. A few years before I left the Orchard Group, I revealed my position to our senior leadership team and a few of our board members. A short time later I revealed it to additional lead pastors of our East Coast churches. Many held the same position but were also holding it privately. We talked about how and when we could start letting our affirmation of the LGBTQ+ population be known.

When I think about it now, the main thing holding us back was money. Evangelical churches that became LGBTQ+ affirming lost about 20 percent of their people and 25 percent of their income. It took about eighteen months to get back to where you were before you announced your change in position, and there was a lot of turmoil in those intervening months. All of us were afraid we would lose money and people if our churches came out as open and affirming of gay relationships. I knew our overall ministry would take a huge financial hit, far greater than 20 percent. Too much of our financial support came from conservative churches. I did not encourage these pastors to take a stand on principle, because I wasn't ready to take a stand, either. I thought it was all right to wait until the social environment had changed a bit more.

That my decision continued to marginalize LGBTQ+ people was only part of the problem. In the final analysis, my decision was self-serving. By refusing to take a stand, I was holding a public position that cost me absolutely nothing. At that point I was not planning to come out as transgender. As long as I stayed in the closet, I could remain quiet on the subject and keep every bit of power and comfort to which I had grown accustomed. I should have been suspicious of just how easy my life was. People who truly allow their conscience to lead will find themselves on a more difficult path. At some level, I did know I was taking the easy way, and it left a gnawing discomfort in my gut.

I imagine most male religious leaders are as blind to the convenience of their theological positions on LGBTQ+ issues and women's rights as I was to mine. You don't wake up in the morning doing an internal examination for signs of privilege. The challenge has to come from outside. The problem is that few of us welcome being challenged from the outside. I know I certainly didn't. Plus, you do not come up with these conservative positions on your own. They are handed to you by people you trust, good people who are as blind to their privilege as you are to yours. But there is that gnawing discomfort, vague but unmistakable, that comes to you in the quiet moments and begs for your attention. That is the voice I ignored. Refusing to receive its message is a decision I regret.

Whenever a pastoral counseling client is struggling with a big decision, I always ask a question I first learned from Jungian analyst James Hollis: "If you say yes to this, will the decision enhance your life, or diminish it?" It is a simple question, and most often it is the clarifying question my client needs. It is a far better question than the one we commonly ask ourselves: "Will this decision make my life harder or will it make my life easier?" If you are looking to satisfy your soul, asking whether a decision will make your life harder or easier is the wrong question to ask. We can either spend our lives searching for comfort or we can spend our lives searching for meaning. Rarely will the two lead to the same conclusion.

If I had asked myself that same question when we were deciding whether or not to be public about our affirmation of the LGBTQ+ population, I would have known the answer almost immediately. It was diminishing my life not to publicly support LGBTQ+ people. It was not a position of intellectual integrity nor did it address the growing call for authenticity coming from my own soul. Yet that was the position I publicly held. I had a lot of soul searching to do.

PART II

CHAPTER 8

A Call to Deny

*Of all the liars in the world, sometimes the worst
are our own fears.*

—RUDYARD KIPLING

The first few months in Colorado were a time of recalibration. I arrived without a clear agenda for personal or professional growth. I had stepped down from day-to-day management at the Orchard Group, but at that time I was still serving as CEO. I added the responsibility of preaching regularly at the megachurch where we attended, but it did not provide the adrenaline rush that goes along with taking on a huge new challenge. Professionally, I was comfortable. Personally, I was struggling.

Cathy and I were renting a house and looking for a place to build a home. Early in the spring of 2007, we found the right lot in a small development nestled in the foothills of the Rockies. We put a down payment on the property and started preparing to move into our dream home, a ranch on a private drive with mountain views in three directions. The house had four bedrooms, three bathrooms, a gourmet kitchen, a kitchenette downstairs, and a beautiful study where we would eventually see counseling clients.

We moved into our beautiful new home in September 2007 and entered the last period of calm before the storm of my transition. I was regularly flying back to the city, where our main office was located. I kept a small apartment near our former home and stayed there when I was in the city, about one week a month. Cathy was teaching the third grade, which she did for five years in Colorado before retiring and returning to school to get a master of arts degree in counseling. I began seeing a therapist in Denver who specialized in gender dysphoria, still hoping I could make it through life without transitioning. In addition to not wanting my family to suffer, I was motivated by two other fears.

I was afraid I would not survive a divorce and terrified I would never pass in public as a woman. I was six feet two inches tall and weighed 190 pounds. I had a long nose and protruding larynx. I wore a size forty-two extra-long suit and size twelve shoes. I had nightmares in which I walked down the street as a woman and every single person stopped and stared or jeered as I passed by. I was sure that if I transitioned, those nightmares would become a reality.

One day I asked my Colorado therapist if she thought I could pass as a woman, meaning that people would think I was a cisgender woman. She thought for a long time before answering, "I'm afraid you would not pass. I'm afraid your height will stop you from passing as a cisgender female." I was heartsick. That sealed it for me. I would never consider transitioning. I knew I didn't have the emotional strength to spend the rest of my life listening to derogatory comments.

While I was struggling to remain a man, Cathy and I were getting along okay, but mostly as friends, not lovers. We both continued individual therapy, and a couple of years after moving to Colorado, Cathy's therapist suggested we consider marital counseling. Cathy and I had been married for almost forty years. We had each been in individual therapy for twenty of those years and had worked through a plethora of marriage issues. Was there really a marriage therapist who could help us now? Cathy looked at her therapist as if to say, *You have got to be kidding me.* Her therapist responded, "I know most marriage therapists would not be able to help you, but there is this one person who is brilliant and extremely capable." We made an appointment with Mike, the therapist she recommended, and in our very first session realized he was a master counselor. He told us we could not expect much progress unless we were willing to put every option on the table, including divorce. Was I going to transition? If I did, would it be better if we divorced? We immediately said no to any talk of divorce. Neither Cathy nor I wanted to put splitting up on the table.

I was still as terrified of divorce as I had been when Cathy first mentioned it. From a practical perspective, ending our marriage at our ages would be financially devastating. Besides, we were not at all emotionally prepared to consider such a drastically different future than the one we had envisioned. Mike's help was invaluable, and eventually his words gave us a way forward. Mike knew how hard we were working and how much progress we were making. That meant a lot to both of us. His words in our final session before his retirement will stay with us forever. When I asked how many couples were willing to work as hard as we had worked, Mike said, "One percent." When I asked how many couples had gotten as far as we had in working through our marital issues, he again answered, "One percent."

Whatever the outcome, Mike helped us realize we had done everything we possibly could to make our marriage work while also not abandoning our own individual growth. A marriage is not two halves becoming one whole. It is two whole people creating a new entity—the relationship. The relationship has to be nurtured just like you nurture a child. In fact, it has to be nurtured more than you nurture a child, because a marriage will be a part of your daily life longer than your children will be. But a marriage does not require that you sacrifice your own growth. In fact, a marriage that asks you to compromise your well-being is not a healthy one. A good marriage encourages the evolution of each person in the partnership. Couples who never stop growing as individuals have a stronger likelihood of maintaining a healthy marriage. It will shift significantly over the years but in a way that does not diminish either partner.

We wanted to save our marriage, but with Mike's help we had come to understand that it might not be possible to do so while also taking care of our own individual needs. As painful as it was to realize that possibility, it allowed us to move ahead without carrying the evangelical baggage of believing divorce is always wrong. Mike had retired and we were on our own, but we felt we had the tools necessary to figure out a way forward.

Cathy and I both loved Colorado, and once Jael and her family moved to the Denver area, we enjoyed it even more. Two of our three children were in the region, along with three of our five grandchildren. Jonathan and his family were living in Brooklyn, and my regular trips back to New York were providing ample opportunity to spend time with his family. On free weekends, Cathy and I hiked together in Rocky Mountain National Park and began drawing up plans for retirement.

Years before, Cathy and I both wanted to become educated as counselors and decided that after she finished teaching, she would go back to school to get her master of arts degree in counseling. That is when I enrolled in a doctor of ministry program with a special emphasis in pastoral care. We planned to practice together in retirement and formed our own company to make that possible.

It was a strange time. On one hand, we were acting as if all was well and we were going to move happily into retirement. On the other, we were both in individual counseling and couples therapy, anticipating the possibility of a very different future than the one we had envisioned. It was as though we were living in parallel universes. Then something happened that ripped me to my core and made me realize I had to make a decision.

In 2010, the sixth and final season of my favorite television show of all time came to a close. *Lost* was about a group of airplane crash survivors marooned on an island in the Pacific. In one episode of the final season, the protagonist realizes he had been called by the God figure to die. Cathy was gone for the night and I was home alone when I saw the episode, and I had a sudden epiphany that dropped me to my knees. I, too, was called to die. It swept over me like an emotional tsunami. My face turned deep red and I felt like God was saying: "Are you seeing this? Do you realize this is also your story? Do you know I am calling you to die just as Jack [the protagonist] has to die?" I wept for three hours before falling into a fitful sleep. I awoke at 4:00 a.m. and wept all the way to dawn. I knew, beyond a shadow of a doubt, that I was being called to leave my existing life and move into the unknown, and it was terrifying.

For months I held what happened that night to myself, frightened of talking with Cathy or anyone else about the certainty of the call. I did not want to admit it to myself, let alone admit it to Cathy. I didn't even tell my therapist about it. I needed to sit alone with the raw emotional power it unleashed within me. I had never experienced anything like that night, the blood rushing through my body, my heart racing. I had a similar feeling a couple of years earlier, when Carol, my friend in New Hampshire, said to me, "You know you can't go back." But it was nothing like this. This was what I would call a true "come to Jesus" moment. I can still watch a recording of that episode, or any episode of the final season of *Lost*, and dissolve in tears. We are a narrative-based species. We don't sleep without dreaming, and we don't dream in mathematical equations. We dream in stories. A story has the power to change a person's life, and that story upended mine.

In retrospect, that evening in the living room watching *Lost* was my turning point. It was the moment when my once-before-a-time became my once-upon-a-time. It was months before I told anyone what happened that winter night. I had been profoundly changed.

Until then, being transgender was something to fight and, ultimately, triumph over. Fighting my gender dysphoria was where I put all of my energy. Suddenly, I was no longer in a war against being transgender. I was in a war to deny a clear call to transition. When I did tell Cathy about it, I also told her about a letter I had written to my therapist shortly after watching the show, explaining all the reasons I could never transition. But with each protestation I could feel the foundation cracking. Staying in denial was not working. I had been called, and I knew it. Though I kept insisting I would never transition, I could see Cathy growing more and more distant. I wasn't sure if it was me pulling away from her, or Cathy pulling away from me, or both of us moving in the direction of that which terrified us the most, to the knowledge that our marriage was not going to survive.

We took a short vacation to Oregon and though we loved the trip, we took it as friends, not lovers. It was the first vacation we had ever taken where we were not intimate with each other. I wanted to be, but I remember sitting alone in the library of our little hotel thinking, *It's like I've lost the combination to the lock. I can't access my desire.*

Shortly after returning home, I found the courage to go to my therapist for the first time as Paula. I had an evening appointment. I changed in my car in the parking lot of her office building and found the outside door locked. As I was about to return to my car in a panic, a cleaner opened the door and said in broken English, "That's a pretty dress." I didn't know if she was giving me a compliment or mocking me. I felt awkward and uncomfortable and remember little of the session other than the interaction with the cleaning lady.

About once a month I began dressing as Paula for my therapy sessions. I always changed in the car and changed back immediately after the session was over. I parked in a remote corner of the parking lot and only scheduled sessions for the evening hours. I was not ready to go out in public during the daytime dressed as Paula. With each session I became a little less terrified.

Cathy knew I was taking clothes with me and dressing as Paula, but we did not talk about it much. It was probably one of the least communicative times of our marriage. We had never shied away from talking about difficult subjects, but we were exhausted. When we talked about our struggles in marriage therapy every other week, we usually talked on the way home from the sessions, an hour-and-a-half drive. Those were some of the most difficult conversations of our entire marriage. Cathy and I could both feel the direction in which we were moving, but when we talked about it, we both quickly dropped into despair. We could not find common ground. She wanted a husband, and I was unhappy as a man. During the last half hour home, we would ride in silence and not talk about it again until our next session two weeks later.

For eighteen months we both lived in the liminal space between being husband and wife and being longtime friends. I do not have many memories of the time between the summer of 2010 and the spring of 2012. I have counseling clients who do not remember anything about long periods of their childhood years. Their lack of memories tells me there are many hidden wounds in those years. I do not remember much about that twenty-month period, and I am confident there are hidden wounds in those years for me, too. Other than going to therapy and marriage counseling, every other part of my life was fairly routine, as it had been since we moved to Colorado.

I traveled a lot, speaking all over the United States. I worked with the television network and the magazine. I mountain biked and ran and hiked in the mountains. I preached regularly in two megachurches, one in Pennsylvania and one in Colorado, and I chaired the boards of several of the new churches we had started over the previous two years.

I can tell you everything that happened during that time period at the television network, magazine, and the Orchard Group. I can tell you what I was preaching at the two megachurches. I can tell you my exercise routine and spout off the specifications of the mountain bike I purchased. But I cannot tell you how I *felt* about my marriage or my internal struggle with the call I had received in 2010. I remember facts, not feelings.

The truth is that I do not want to remember those months. They were too painful. Slowly coming to an awareness that you cannot stave off the inevitable is terrifying. It is exactly as I describe my awakening that night I was watching *Lost*. I knew I had been called to die.

In the hero's journey, an ordinary citizen is called onto an extraordinary journey on the road of trials. Initially she rejects the call because, after all, it is the road of trials. But she knows she has been called and is now miserable because she has rejected the call. That is when a spiritual guide comes into the hero's life and gives her the courage to accept the call and go on the road of trials. That is what this period of time felt like to me. I was rejecting a call I could not deny. I was trying to go about my daily life, but every time I was with Cathy, I knew the painful truth. The embers of our marriage were dying. We both knew it. It was an unspoken awful bond between us. I had rejected the call, but I knew my current life was no longer sustainable.

I do know who the spiritual guide was who finally gave me the strength to accept the call on the hero's journey. It was Cathy. I had mentioned to her that my therapist had told me she would write a letter of introduction to a physician who specialized in cross-sex hormone therapy. The therapist suggested it was possible a low dose of hormones and antiandrogens might help calm me. When I told Cathy, she not only gave me permission to go to the doctor and begin hormones but she also said, "You need to do this. You need to know if it will help you or not." Cathy was devastated and hurt but also convinced. Beneath all of her emotions was the truth. To love me meant to let me go.

With my letter from my therapist in hand, I made an appointment with Anna, a physician in Denver who specializes in cross-sex hormone therapy. At my first appointment, I could barely contain my glee. Though I was frightened and understood the gravity of my decision, my overall reaction was one of hope, not fear.

On May 31, 2012, I began taking a low dose of spironolactone to hinder the production of testosterone. I also began taking a low dose of transdermal estrogen. I noticed no changes for the first six weeks. Then quite suddenly, significant changes became apparent. I lost muscle mass. My skin became thinner and softer. Fat disappeared from my waist and migrated to my hips and upper arms. Breasts began to develop. When I went to my physician two months after starting my regimen, she said, "I thought a low dose of hormones might enable you to remain a man a little longer. But you are going to have to make some big decisions. At the rate of change your body is experiencing, it will not be long before it is obvious you are fundamentally changed. Paula, your body has been craving this stuff." That conversation took place in July. I drove home from the doctor's office knowing I did not want to stop taking hormones, no matter how rapidly the changes were taking place in my body.

In a little over two years, my feelings had come full circle. Until my epiphany while watching *Lost*, I had always been certain I would be able to get through life without transitioning. From the time I watched that show to the summer of 2012, my progression from opposition to openness was gradual. It was also excruciating. Mike had been right. Cathy and I had worked extraordinarily hard to figure out how to make our marriage work, but we were beginning to know the end was near. I knew the hormones were confirming the truth that I was transgender. I was experiencing the loss of testosterone as a blessing, and the arrival of estrogen as a godsend. I still could not say it out loud, but I did not doubt that I had been called to transition.

I came home that day and told Cathy what the physician had said. I told her I was going to wait a few days and decide what to do. Cathy immediately said, "You know you can't stop. You are so much happier and so much more at peace since you started taking hormones. It terrifies me to think of what this means, but you can't stop." I knew it took great love for Cathy to speak those words, because in saying them, she was ultimately acknowledging that we were at a turning point. Neither one of us was ready to admit it yet, but the die had been cast.

Cathy had always been kind and understanding in working with me through the difficulties of being transgender. We were both woefully ignorant in the beginning, but over time we had figured out how to make our marriage work in spite of that great obstacle.

Cathy is a fiercely devoted woman. She is devoted to her children, to her grandchildren, and to me. Most people find Cathy to be quiet and unassuming, a private person whose inner life remains a mystery. The word I hear most often to describe Cathy is *sweet*. Cathy is beautiful and petite and kind, but if you know her, she is not always sweet. Cathy is determined. She was determined to be a good wife and mother and, early in our relationship, a good evangelical Christian. It was understandable. Her entire family were evangelical Christians and remain so. Early in our relationship Cathy rarely questioned evangelical theology, but within one or two years of marrying, she began to question the hard-and-fast rules of the evangelical world. When we moved to Long Island, she began questioning even more, and when she became a public school teacher and began spending most of her time outside the evangelical bubble, Cathy's separation from evangelicalism accelerated. She was done with evangelical judgmentalism.

While Cathy's faith was moving toward a broader expression of Christianity, her interest in social justice and psychological health was increasing. She attended an African American church and began to talk about having a second career as a counselor, helping sexual abuse survivors and those wounded by toxic faith. As long as the children were at home, they were her first priority, but after they left, she finished two master's degrees and switched careers from teaching to counseling.

Through all of these changes, Cathy remained committed to me and to our marriage, but her commitment was no longer based on evangelical convictions. It was more dynamic, recognizing that she could not love me well if she did not also love herself well. When it came to me being transgender, one of Mike's comments at the end of our time together was profoundly helpful to both Cathy and me. When he told us that we had worked harder and gotten further than 99 percent of his clients, Mike ended by saying, "And that is the great tragedy. In spite of all of your hard work, if transitioning genders is the final outcome, you will be a lesbian and Cathy will not."

Cathy and I both always believed the truth would set us free. But the truth can be difficult to discern and to speak. She was beginning to discern the truth of Mike's observation and the difficult reality of what it meant for our future. When Cathy said she knew I could not stop taking hormones, she was speaking a truth she did not want to know.

CHAPTER 9

Telling Our Children

Let yourself be gutted. Let it open you. Start here.

—CHERYL STRAYED

Rituals mark the chapters of our lives. Rituals for graduation, marriage, the arrival of children, and retirement are celebratory affairs. Others mark more difficult chapters, like divorce rituals, designed to end a marriage with respect and dignity. But there are no rituals for telling your family you are transgender. You are on your own.

I wanted my children to know I had always loved being their father, and the years when they were at home were the most peaceful of my life. During those years I thought it was possible to make it through life without transitioning. Fatherhood gave me a reprieve from the battle I had been waging. I loved providing my children with the emotional, spiritual, and physical nurture they needed to grow into themselves. I loved that Cathy and I had very different personalities, which allowed us to parent in our own unique ways while maintaining a united front.

Since I did not think I was going to transition, there had been no reason to tell our children I was transgender. At the time we finally decided to tell them, there were only a handful of people who knew. All were therapists, including the friends we had told. My gender identity was private. Cathy and I feared that if the information got out, my career would be over instantly. It would not matter whether or not I was planning to transition. Just the knowledge I was transgender would have been enough to get me fired and prevent me from working in the evangelical world.

Once we began to discern where life was headed, Cathy and I had several conversations about how and when to tell our children. They were all in their thirties, married, and had their own children. We never even thought about telling them until I went on hormones. Even then we were hoping a low dose of hormones might be enough to settle my longing. When the doctor told me that my body was changing more quickly than she had expected, Cathy and I began to understand the urgency of talking with Jonathan, Jael, and Jana.

When you raise healthy adult children, who differentiate yet remain connected, you can expect honesty to be a valued family touchstone. You also know honesty is at the top of the family's chain of command. Anyone is allowed to claim it to frame a conversation. We had not yet settled on a plan for telling our children, when our children took control of the conversation. Jana called Cathy in late November 2012 and said, "Something is wrong, Mom. You've got to come clean. It's been obvious for months that something is going on between you and Dad." Relieved that Jana had initiated the painful process, Cathy said, "All right, Jana. You are right. It's been tough, but we don't want to tell you on the phone. We want you to be here together." Jana said she would talk with her siblings.

When she called back an hour later, she said, "Jael and I will be there in two hours. We talked with Jonathan and he wants Jael and me to tell him what is going on." Cathy said okay and Jana and Jael arrived two hours later.

As I sat in an oversize chair almost big enough for two, Cathy and the girls sat on the couch, a few feet away. That chair is my favorite in the house. It is usually a place of comfort. It is where I turn when I am hurting and need to heal. But now the chair brought no comfort at all. As I spoke, it felt like my voice was coming from someplace other than my body. I told them what I was going to say would be difficult to hear. No, neither of their parents was ill, but there was going to be a massive change that would be difficult for everyone. I said as evenly as I could, "I am transgender and have known it since I was three or four years old." I burst into tears. Almost immediately Jael came over to sit with me. She said, "We love you. It's okay. We will be here for you. We're not going anywhere." Jana joined her and the girls sat on either side of me on the arms of the easy chair. For quite a while the three of us sat silently, hugging.

I then did what I ended up doing scores of times over the next few years. I explained in detail what it means to be transgender. I said I had been on hormones for six months and that it was increasingly looking like I would transition within the next few years. I wept. Jael and Jana had a lot of questions, and I did my best to answer them. After talking for an hour or so, I showed the girls a video I had recently watched of an address by Lana Wachowski, one of the directors of the *Matrix* films. She had received a Human Rights Campaign award and, in her acceptance speech, spoke eloquently about the struggles of growing up transgender. The twenty minutes we watched the video gave me time to recover my equilibrium. I was feeling outside of my body, as though I were on the far side of the room, looking through a thin tube at my girls on the other side. Throughout the conversation, Cathy sat quietly, answering when asked specific questions but otherwise letting the girls take the lead.

I really do not remember how long Jael and Jana were at the house. I know that when they left, I was completely spent and sat staring at the walls for a couple of hours. Cathy sat quietly with me. Everyone was in shock. There had been absolutely nothing to prepare my children for this news—nothing. I had never exhibited the tiniest of feminine mannerisms or behavior. I had never talked about questioning my gender. I had been the quintessential father: corporate CEO, sometimes confidant, the rock of the family. I had played the role well, and none of our children had a hint of awareness of what was coming.

Jana called Jonathan and told him some of the conversation, but not enough for him to truly understand the magnitude of what I had revealed. After talking with Jonathan, Jael and Jana told their husbands. It was an extremely difficult day for both of my daughters, but that is their story to tell.

Jael and Jana did not pull away from me. They stayed close for several months, wanting to be sure I was all right. They invited me to their houses and took me to lunch. I was still living as Paul, and we had no plans to tell their children, because I was still not sure I would transition. I was grateful they remained close.

Since Jonathan lived in New York, I was planning to fly there the week after the girls came to the house. I would travel to Brooklyn after speaking at a church in Kentucky. It felt so strange to speak at the church, to be acting as if nothing had changed or was going to change. The church was in eastern Kentucky. I had spoken there frequently since I was in my early twenties. The pastor had been the program director at the radio station where I worked. After I preached that Sunday, we talked of old times and disc jockeys with whom we had worked. While we were eating lunch, I got a text from Jonathan telling me he did not want me to come to New York until the whole family could come. As I drove back to the Cincinnati airport, I was crying so hard I pulled off the side of the highway to catch my breath. Instead of going to New York, I flew back to Denver. When I got back home late that night, I sat in my easy chair and stared at the clay pots above the kitchen cabinets. Those clay pots were becoming friends, repositories for my accumulating pain. I went through the next week in a fog.

The following week Cathy, Jael, and Jana flew with me to New York City, so we could talk with Jonathan and his wife, Jubi, and process the information as a family. The girls' husbands stayed home with their children.

As soon as we arrived at Jonathan and Jubi's Brooklyn apartment, we all sat down in the living room. An awkward silence permeated the room. Jonathan and I were in two facing chairs. Cathy, Jubi, Jael, and Jana were on the couch between us. I told Jonathan everything I had told the girls a couple of weeks earlier. After a period of stunned silence, Jonathan started speaking about his feelings of betrayal. How could I have withheld such critical information from him? Weren't we the family that was honest about everything? Hadn't we agreed to always bring up the tough subjects and work our way through them together? I listened. I needed to hear what he was thinking and feeling. He went on for more than an hour. Jubi was mostly quiet. The girls spoke occasionally, usually to clarify something I had said. I was not my usual articulate self. I was struggling to speak at all. The rest of the day was awful, the air filled with anger, sadness, and silence.

I began to dissociate and knew it was not going to be helpful to anyone if I sat there with a blank expression on my face. I thought about the stages of working through conflict. A lot of families live in pseudocommunity, never digging beneath the surface. No one talks about Grandpa's narcissism, or Big Sister's addiction, or any of the difficult truths no one wants to confront. It is a mature family that commits to moving beyond pseudocommunity to chaos, the next stage in creating genuine community. Someone finds the courage to say the emperor has no clothes, and mayhem ensues. Most families retreat to pseudocommunity. At the moment, it's easier. But if the family does not shy away from remaining in the chaos, truth is aired, and problems are confronted. The next stage might be the most difficult. After chaos comes emptiness. Everyone is spent, and no one can see a way forward. As I thought about how we were all feeling that day, I knew we had reached the stage of emptiness and that we would be there for a long time. Would it be weeks? Months? Years? At the time, I was hoping our family could get back to normal within several months. I was still not grasping that we were going to have to create a new normal, and it was going to take years.

If a family is willing to work through the chaos and emptiness, eventually there is a light at the end of the tunnel. Finally, the family's shattered pseudocommunity is replaced by genuine community, and a family's bonds are stronger than ever.

At the moment, it felt like we would never move beyond emptiness. What I remember most was the tortured look on Jonathan's face as he said he had lost his father, and the concern on Jubi's face as she watched her husband struggle. The rest of the trip is a blur. In fact, I do not remember much about the next month. Because there are pictures, I know we had Christmas at our house. I know I played with the grandchildren and did not talk much with the adults. It was a lost holiday season, a month none of my family should ever have had to experience. Everyone was in excruciating pain, and it had all been sourced by me.

I cannot speak for other transgender individuals, but I wish there had been another pathway for me. I wish I could have gotten through life without transitioning. I wish the low dose of estrogen and anti-androgens had given my body the help it needed to allow me to continue living as a man. My transition caused too much pain for the people I love. From my perspective, the best solution would be to discover what makes a person transgender and correct it before it begins. I believe its cause is likely genetic or prenatal or a combination of both. Whatever the genesis of gender dysphoria, I wish I could have lived my life without having to struggle with it. I wish I had not always felt I had been born the wrong gender. At the current pace of study, it will be a long time before we understand much about what causes a person to be transgender. Transgender people comprise only 0.58 percent of the population. Not many research dollars are poured into the well-being of our community. Maybe someday we will know more and be able to relieve the suffering of individuals and families. Someday.

As we entered the New Year in January 2013, we were a fragile family. Would we fracture irreparably, or would we make it through? We all wanted our family to survive and become stronger, but we were all having difficulty seeing our way out of the abyss.

After our visit to Brooklyn, Jonathan pretty much disappeared. For the next fifteen months, we were rarely in contact. The girls were staying close, providing me with life-giving support. It was much later that they each took their leave as they worked through the difficulty of my transition. It was devestating to lose contact with my children. Yet every single time, I felt the best response was to give them the space they needed to work through their grief. I did not express anger or retaliate. I did not reach out to them until they reached out to me.

Through the first half of 2013, Jonathan took my calls, but the contact was superficial. He had just started a church. Complicating that reality was the fact that the church had been started through the Orchard Group. I had not been the one to initiate his work with an Orchard Group church; the new CEO had started the process. But Jonathan was now in the same place Cathy had been for the better part of four decades. He had information he could not talk about because of what it would do to my livelihood and his. It was a profoundly difficult period for Jonathan and Jubi. Jonathan wrote about the experience in a book released in late 2018.

She's My Dad was published right before Jonathan and I spoke for TEDWomen in Palm Springs. There are not many resources for the family members of transgender people, and Jonathan's book was an honest and raw account of how he worked through the news that I was transgender. I wrote responses to five of the chapters. I read each of the chapters as they were completed and wrote my responses immediately after reading what Jonathan had written. He did not hide his pain. Reading each chapter was difficult. Though it is a very redemptive book, it is still hard for me to read Jonathan's words. So much of what he wrote was about the bond that existed between the two of us. I liked his description of our relationship, and I liked the father about whom he wrote. But it was difficult to read. I had left that good man behind.

In so many ways Paul is gone, yet here I sit in the great room, writing at the kitchen counter, staring at my reflection in the bay window. It is dusk, and my reflection is clear. I see a woman with curly brown hair, a red sweater, and a gray top. Just a woman. What does she have to do with the man Jonathan wrote about? I'm not sure.

It is not unusual to look back on life and see the stages through which we have grown. But at the end of life, we can still recognize ourselves as the person we once were. We see the continuity. In my case, there is more discontinuity than continuity.

When Jonathan took his leave, he found a good therapist and did the work he needed to do to move ahead. I had been to New York City a few times during the period in which we were not communicating, but I had stayed at a hotel and did not see Jonathan or his family. In May 2015 I was scheduled to return to New York and I asked Jonathan if it would be all right if I stayed at his apartment. He said yes. I arrived at their Brooklyn apartment not knowing whether anyone was home or not. I had a key to their downstairs door, and I texted Jonathan to ask if I should use that key to come in. He texted back a single word: **Nope.**

I thought he had changed his mind about seeing me. My heart sunk. Then he texted again: **Just come in the front door. I'm here.** As soon as I walked through the door, I knew he was ready to reconcile. I saw it on his face. It was warm and accepting. The sparkle was back in his eyes. We engaged in small talk for a good long while before he suggested we walk down to Brooklyn Bridge Park. As we walked, he talked about his therapy process, his anger, hurt, and disappointment. His tone was one of reconciliation.

We sat down on a huge, wide staircase overlooking the East River and the Downtown Manhattan Heliport. As we talked, three identical Sikorsky helicopters circled and landed, accompanied by several V-22 Ospreys. I said, "Obama just came to town. That's his Sikorsky, two decoys, and an escort." Jonathan chuckled and said, "Some things don't change. You are still the person who knows everything flying in the sky." It was the first time he had acknowledged that there was any continuity between my old life and my new life. I was encouraged.

He told me about his therapy process, and how he had come to the conclusion that he wanted to have a relationship with me because I was, in fact, his father. We walked back to the house and that is when I met his girls. Jonathan wrote about that beautifully in his book.

Asha and Lyla were sitting at the dining room table, coloring. They felt awkward until I began talking with them, and they invited me into their bedroom where they showed me the new clothes they had gotten. Then Lyla, without hesitation or embarrassment, said, "I do have one question for you: Do you still have a penis?" If there had been any tension in the room, it was immediately gone. Everyone laughed, including Jonathan and Jubi. I explained to the girls that you don't ask a transgender person that question, because it is private. They understood and began showing me more of their new clothes. Then Asha told me they had decided to give me a new name. I could tell they were proud of themselves for having thought of it. Asha said, "We're going to call you GramPaula!" Lyla said, "What do you think?" I hugged them both tightly and said, "I love it, girls. I love it!" The entire trip was as redemptive and upbeat as the previous trip had been awful. Jonathan had worked through the worst of his pain, and I knew we were going to be all right.

Occasionally Jonathan will talk about that first year, usually when we are speaking together at a conference or on a podcast. He doesn't talk about it much when it is just the two of us. Jonathan took his leave in a way and time that were right for him. He gets a lot of grief from some people who read his book. They feel he was too tough on me. When I read the manuscript, I did not think he was too tough. Jonathan is my only son. We had a wonderful father-and-son relationship. I irrevocably changed that relationship. He had a right to be angry. That we have done a TED Talk and other TED events together, as well as numerous podcasts and television shows and conferences, is a testament to his forgiveness and desire to help other families going through similar experiences. I have great respect for my son.

My daughters were there for me from the beginning. Their encouragement in those early years was critically important. Jael has always been strong. From the day I first set eyes on her at JFK Airport when she arrived from India, I saw fire in that two-month-old little girl's eyes. I knew she was a survivor. From the beginning, her fierce eyes said, "Don't mess with me."

Jael needed that strength and her streak of independence to survive as a Brown child in a White family, an Indian child in an American family, an adopted child with two siblings who were biologically ours. Hers was not an easy childhood. After she finished college, Jael, much to my surprise, became the children's pastor at a new church we were starting in lower Manhattan. It was my first chance to see her at work as an adult. She was innovative, self-motivated, hardworking, and intelligent. It was a gift to be able to see Jael in that setting, since at home she was the middle child, with all the encumbrances of being the middle child. She never demanded as much attention as Jonathan and Jana. Jael always went with the flow. Now she was creating the flow.

Shortly after Cathy and I moved to Colorado, Jael moved to work with a megachurch in the Phoenix area. She married not long after that, and she and Kijana, her husband, had a daughter, Trista. After Trista was born, they decided to move to Colorado to be closer to our family. Kijana is a senior software architect and was easily able to find a job. Jael became an elementary school teacher and then a school administrator. She has advanced quickly in her career. Trista is a precious child, bright-eyed and curious. She had very little difficulty adjusting to my transition. She was five at the time, and most children six and under adjust pretty quickly to the transition of a parent or grandparent.

Jana is our youngest child. When she was in high school, she was outgoing and popular and had an uncanny ability to get adults to give her what she wanted. Jana did not lack confidence, whether it was cajoling teachers to sign slips to let her out of class, or convincing police officers that the bread that had just fallen out of her shirt had not, in fact, been stolen from the doorstep of the bakery where she and her friends were sitting. (She did work at the bakery. But it was also well after midnight. And they were, in fact, stealing the bread.) The police officers just smiled and drove away. Jana has charisma.

I was surprised when Jana, too, became a children's pastor at one of the churches affiliated with the Orchard Group. She, too, was hardworking, innovative, and productive. I loved watching her at work. She processed information quickly and became bored when life was moving too slowly. She left ministry when she grew exhausted fighting the misogyny inherent in evangelical churches. She is now the owner of a catering business in Denver, where she lives with her twin daughters.

Jana was extremely supportive in the year after I told my children I was transgender. We got together for dinner regularly, and she called to check in on me constantly, serving as a great source of encouragement. In August 2016 I moved into a studio apartment in Denver, about ten minutes away from Jana. She had gone through a divorce that spring and was working through her own turmoil. I expected to see Jana and her twins a good bit while I was living in Denver, but after she made an early visit to my apartment, I did not see her again for the next thirteen months—the entire time I lived in Denver. She was doing her work of differentiation. I understood.

Ava and Macy, Jana's twins, were only three when I transitioned, so they have no memory of me as Paul. As far as they remember, things have always been this way. The rest of my grandchildren talk easily about when I was still their grandfather. For all five granddaughters, my transition was no big deal. That truth has been a blessing for us all.

Jael was staunchly and steadfastly supportive from the day I first told her I was transgender until almost seven years later, when she finally took her leave for a short period. I can only imagine how she must have felt. As if it weren't enough to be a Brown child in an American family growing up in a White New York City suburb. Now she had to contend with the fact that her father transitioned genders. But Jael is fiercely loyal, and she has been a strong support from the beginning. My transition was not fair to Jael, Jana, or Jonathan. It was not fair to Cathy. It was not fair to anyone. It just was what it was.

CHAPTER 10

Time before a Time

The only thing more unthinkable than leaving was staying;
the only thing more impossible than staying was leaving.

—ELIZABETH GILBERT, *EAT, PRAY, LOVE*

After telling my children I was transgender, the early days of 2013 brought a measure of normalcy as I led a retreat of contributing editors for the magazine I served and helped lead an annual pastor's retreat in Miami Beach. I began traveling and speaking at churches again and working intensely with my therapist in Colorado to figure out if there was a way I could avoid transitioning.

After seeing how Jonathan had responded, I began to see more clearly how the Orchard Group might respond if I told them I was transgender. But I had a lifetime of entitlement under my belt. I still thought that somehow everything would turn out all right. People knew my character. They would give me the time I needed to wind down my work and ease into a new life. My perspective was spectacularly self-referential, which is pretty typical for White men.

My plan was to tell my fellow workers I was transgender and that I thought there was a distinct possibility, though not yet a probability, that I would eventually transition. I would suggest that for the next twelve months, I would continue my work unchanged, and the information would be kept at the board and senior staff level, a total of about fifteen people.

After twelve months, I would stop traveling and speaking on behalf of the ministry and would confine my work to mentoring pastors and leading church boards. Then after twenty-four months, if I still felt the need to transition, I would leave the Orchard Group. I thought it was a workable plan. At the time, twenty-one states had prohibitions against firing transgender workers, though they all had exemptions for religious corporations. I was pretty sure our staff and board were sophisticated enough to understand the circumstances and agree to the plan. They knew my character and value to the ministry. They would at least follow the spirit of the law, though they were not legally compelled to follow its letter. Surely they would keep me employed for another two years.

If I transitioned after that time, I knew my days with the Orchard Group were over. A significant percentage of our financial support came from conservative churches, and they would not tolerate the ministry keeping a transgender person on staff. But I thought my plan was workable.

Rose-colored glasses is not an adequate metaphor to describe my naivete. The plan might have been feasible in a secular corporation, though even there it would have been ludicrous to think board members were going to keep that kind of information to themselves for twenty-four months.

Through the spring of 2013 I continued to travel and speak, including preaching for my last men's retreat. I had never felt comfortable speaking at men's retreats. More than any other environment, they were reminders of how uncomfortable I felt as a man. Evangelical men's retreats are a world unto themselves, rooted in the conviction that God placed men in authority over women. Men's retreats do little to encourage introspection. They are not the venues of storytellers and poets. They are places to hear the hard teaching of evangelicalism about salvation and enemies and warfare and the need to protect conservative American values. Men's retreats are often long on nationalistic spirit and short on humility.

The last men's retreat for which I spoke was in Florida on a cold and windy March weekend. For reasons I do not understand, I was very much at peace. Maybe it was because I knew I was nearing the end. Or maybe it was the strength born of my conviction that living authentically is sacred and holy and for the greater good. I was not intimidated by the environment. I was ready to speak into it.

I enjoyed my first evening with the men, and when I woke up the next morning, I went for a long run along the perimeter of an orange grove. The sandy soil was like running on the beach, rewarding great effort with little progress. It was cold and the wind was biting through my sweatshirt. I had prepared a sermon on prayer. Since I memorize all of my sermons, I went over the talk as I ran in the brisk morning air. I forgot about the chill and settled into a rhythm that carried me all the way through the run. I almost never include videos or graphics in my sermons, but this time I was going to use a video of Lisa Kelly of Celtic Woman singing a portion of "The Deer's Cry," otherwise known as "St. Patrick's Breastplate." In the hour before the session, I double-checked to make sure the tech crew had the video cued and I went over my sermon one last time.

I spoke about the importance of trusting life's flow. I told the men about a kayak I used to launch on the Connetquot River, just north of the Great South Bay, about a mile from my Long Island home. If I put the kayak in the river when the tide was coming in, I had trouble rowing out into the bay. Riding against the flow, I was moving at about one mile per hour. If I put the kayak in the water when the tide was going out, I could row five or six miles per hour. It is easier to go with the flow.

In the last half of the message I talked about the importance of offering forgiveness with the flow, not against it. Some of us forgive too early, particularly those of us who have always had a great need for affirmation. Others forgive far too late. I admitted I was someone who tended to forgive too early, before I really understood what had happened and the full effect it had on me. When you have a narcissistic parent, you know your parent will never request forgiveness, so your life will be easier if you just forgive and move on. But forgiveness that comes too soon is cheap forgiveness. It is not bestowing grace; it is maintaining a superficial relationship.

You really cannot forgive someone until there has been a figurative trial, with briefs for the prosecution and briefs for the defense. Only after a full presentation of the evidence can a verdict be rendered. And only after a verdict is rendered can you set aside that verdict and offer forgiveness. As I was going over the sermon in the orange grove that morning, I wondered if my daughters were forgiving me too early. Didn't they feel the same sense of betrayal Jonathan felt? Didn't they also feel frustrated that I had kept this information from them for so long? What Jonathan said was true. We were the kind of family that always told the truth and worked through problems together. I had withheld the truth.

After I told the girls I was transgender on that November day, I could tell the overriding feeling they had was wanting to make sure I was all right. We teach our daughters to defer to the needs of others. It is not always a healthy instruction. Girls are taught that they are not allowed to express anger, but boys are told anger is an acceptable male emotion. Jonathan was angry when I came out to him, and he gave himself permission to be angry. My girls were quick to forgive. But I knew they had to be feeling the same anger and abandonment. That is one of the reasons I knew they might go through their own periods of separation at a later time, after they knew I was all right.

In the sermon I said, "When the time comes that we understand what has happened and the damage that has been done, why would we still choose to forgive? We forgive so we can move on. Unfortunately, when we are angry, we do not want to move on. The food is tasty at the feast of anger. But there is a problem if you remain too angry for too long. The food you are devouring at the feast of anger is you. The longer you stay at the feast of anger, the more of yourself you devour. Ultimately, you forgive so you can move on."

I was surprised how quiet the men became as I spoke. This was not the kind of message they were accustomed to hearing at a men's retreat. But as I looked around the audience, there were a lot of tears. These men wanted someone to break through to their hearts. There was a holy silence in the room. I had preached with passion and conviction that prayer can center us in the moment and take us from a place of fear to a place of calm. It was one of the few moments during that entire year when I truly believed all would be well. As I ended the sermon and played the video of St. Patrick's famous prayer, I found great comfort in the abiding faith that was nurturing me through the most difficult period of my life.

I left the retreat and drove to Orlando, where I stayed at one of my favorite boutique hotels and ate dinner at one of my favorite restaurants. That night I watched a recording of the twenty-fifth anniversary presentation of the Broadway musical *Les Misérables*. I've always loved its theme of forgiveness and redemption. I settled into great peace and slept soundly until dawn. It was a surprising respite in the middle of a great storm.

The next day I received a call from Cathy saying she thought it might be a good idea to find her own place for a few months, and that she and Jael had been out looking at apartments. We had talked about the possibility of separating for a short period, but I didn't think she was really serious. I was devastated. I was sitting at the gate at the Orlando airport waiting for my flight back to Colorado. I walked toward a relatively empty concourse and sat down in a dark corner where I could freely let the tears flow. I could not believe Cathy was looking for an apartment. I could not fathom that Cathy would not be lying next to me in bed, or that her face would not be the first thing I would see each morning. I thought of how empty the house always felt when she was at work, and how hard it would be to spend evenings alone. I even thought of the endless Food Channel television shows she watched and, though I always complained about them, how much I loved watching her enjoy each spirited competition between chefs. It was all of those routine day-to-day interactions I was going to miss. After I boarded the flight, I continued to think about how lonely I would be. The previous day had felt hopeful. This day did not.

I had always hoped, even assumed, Cathy would remain with me if I transitioned. I knew we would no longer be intimate, but I thought we would remain married and would continue to live together. We had both been opposed to considering divorce. I could not imagine Cathy having a change of heart.

When we were in marriage therapy with Mike, he said, "You don't separate to save a marriage. You separate to try out divorce." Now Cathy had asked Jael to help her look for an apartment. Jael had briefly worked in the real estate industry and Cathy needed her help. While I was on a layover between flights, Cathy called to say they had found a nice apartment about thirty minutes from our house.

The next day Cathy began moving furniture and clothes into her new apartment. She was resolved, not excited. There was no joy in moving out of the dream house we had built together. There was just a sad conviction that she needed to get away from the nonstop pain my transition was causing. Maybe a couple of months away would give her the space she needed to clear her head. She had signed a two-month lease and took only the bare essentials with her.

The next morning, I went with Cathy to look at the apartment. It was quite nice, a one-bedroom with an attached garage in a pleasant complex near the university where she was working on her counseling degree. I left the apartment and when I got home, I realized that for the first time in forty-one years, I would be living alone.

Just a week after Cathy moved out, I had an already-scheduled appointment with a surgeon who specializes in facial feminization surgery. I was struggling with Cathy's decision to leave and not sure I wanted to go through with the appointment. Jana graciously accompanied me, and we listened as the doctor explained the differences between male and female faces. The doctor said when someone is transitioning from male to female, the work that needs to be done is often extensive. Testosterone makes major changes to the male face. He also told us that humans are predisposed to see a face as male unless there are clear markers that it is not. Therefore, a face needs to appear distinctly female for a person to be identified as a woman. The doctor then proceeded to measure every part of my face, from my hairline to the tip of my nose to the bottom of my chin. Afterward, we sat down in his office as he explained the procedures used in facial feminization. There could be a brow shave, in which the brow is shaved back so that it does not protrude. They could also reshape the eyes, add cheek implants, reshape the nose, and reshape the jaw. I could see the dollar signs adding up. Then he gave me the good news.

My brow, eyes, and cheeks were totally within female parameters. In fact, every part of my face was within female parameters, with the exception of my nose and larynx. He was recommending rhinoplasty and a tracheal shave, and nothing else. He told me that hormones and electrolysis had already brought about a lot of changes in my body and that continuing my course of hormone therapy would bring about the rest of the changes that needed to take place for my face to be seen as fully feminine. We made arrangements for the surgery to be done when I was off the road for three weeks in July. I was excited, truly excited. I had never had surgery before, and I was pleased that my first one would make my face appear more feminine. For the next few weeks I lived as Paula when I was at home and Paul when I was out of the house. It actually felt consistent with how I viewed myself. It was certainly not sustainable, but I knew it was workable for a season.

I was thrilled when I discovered that the vast majority of the time, I am just seen as a tall woman, not a transgender woman. The loss of testosterone and the effects of estrogen have brought about massive changes in my body. My muscle mass is greatly decreased, my skin is much softer, and my overall appearance is more feminine. My ring size is two sizes smaller, my waist is four inches smaller, and my shoes are two sizes smaller. There is no skeletal change with hormones, so all of those changes are a result of the loss of muscle mass and the migration of body fat.

The first time I ever went out in public as a woman was marked by emotional extremes. I was so frightened, I was shaking. I made eye contact with no one but looked out of the corner of my eye at everyone. Were they staring at me? If so, was it because I was tall, or because I was transgender? I was with Cathy, my daughters, and one of my granddaughters. They were acting completely normal and kept assuring me that no one was paying me any mind, which they saw as a good sign. When we ordered food at a restaurant, the waitress treated me exactly like she treated everyone else at the table. It did not seem to me like I was being "read" as a transgender person, but without the assurance of my family, I was still not convinced I was passing as a female.

As the day wore on and I began to realize I was being blessedly ignored, I was thrilled. It was much later when I realized that being ignored as a woman of a certain age would be my new norm. I was always noticed when I was a male. It was not at all uncommon for me to be waited on in line before the person immediately in front of me. It was as if the person behind the counter did not even see the person in front of me. I would have to say, "Um, there's someone right here." It used to happen a few times a year. Since transitioning, it has never happened.

When I got home after that first day out as a woman, I was ecstatic, probably about as excited as I have ever been. Before that day I always thought I would be subjected to public taunts and derision for being transgender. I thought I would have to avoid going to certain regions of the country or even some countries. In that one afternoon I began to understand my life as a woman would be easier than I had anticipated.

. . .

In early July I attended my final national convention for our denomination. I was a part of a preaching workshop that was well received, and I loved spending time with my many friends in ministry. The week felt completely normal. I was not fully taking in that it would be the last time I would ever see most of these people. I flew home on Sunday and prepared to have surgery the following Tuesday.

The previous fall Jonathan had asked if I wanted to attend the All-Star Game at Citi Field, the Mets' new stadium. I had said I would be interested, but Jonathan never followed up, and since I had not heard much from him since the previous December, I assumed he no longer wanted to attend the game with me. I was surprised when he called in June to talk about going to the game together. I had already scheduled surgery for the week of the game and had a tight speaking schedule for all of August. I needed to be healed from the surgery before I started speaking again. If I did not do surgery that week, I would have to wait until fall. Jonathan was very disappointed.

He wrote about the All-Star Game in his book, and in the end, the game turned out to be a very redemptive day for Jonathan. The fact that I did not attend the game is something for which I still have not forgiven myself. I could have waited until fall for the surgery. It would have been fine. The All-Star Game won't return to Citi Field for a generation. I missed the one chance I had to bring us together for one last ball game before I transitioned.

The story is a sad indicator of how self-centered I was during that time. It has been my observation that most transgender women go through a period in which they are as self-absorbed as a teenage girl. They are excited about becoming a woman, confused by the hormones actively changing their bodies, and consumed by how the world is perceiving them. It would have been just three months that I would have had to wait. Just three months. I wish I had waited.

The morning of the surgery, Cathy drove me to Denver. She had come from her apartment to spend the night at the house. She was planning to stay with me for a few days after the surgery was over. I was nervous but excited. We faced a monumental traffic jam on the way to the hospital and I was afraid I would miss my surgery time. We arrived with a few minutes to spare and were welcomed into the quiet waiting area. A few minutes later we were taken into an examination room where I changed into a hospital gown and placed my clothes in a large wicker basket. Then I walked across the hallway to the operating room and within a couple of minutes I was asleep.

I woke up without pain but with my eyes almost swollen shut. Cathy stayed with me until it was safe for me to leave, and then she got the car as they wheeled me to the hospital entrance. The rest of the day I did not experience much pain. I returned the following morning to have most of the bandages removed, and on our way to the doctor's office, Jonathan called to tell me about the wonderful experience he had the night before at the All-Star Game.

A string of apparently random circumstances had provided him with quite a gift. He was given a seat right behind the players' families, not far from the dugout. He met a colorful fan from Brooklyn who introduced him to people all around the restricted seating area, and he watched a game he thoroughly enjoyed. He offered to take the fan home but got a flat tire on the way back to Brooklyn. Much to his chagrin, the jack in his car did not work. But his new friend stopped a couple of ladies of the evening, who said they could help, and came walking back a few minutes later pulling a gas station jack. Jonathan changed the tire, thanked the girls, took the fan to his apartment, and returned home. The night had been a bizarre and wonderful delight. And the first person he wanted to tell about it was me.

I cried as he excitedly told me what had happened. It was like I was talking to my ten-year-old son again. I was so pleased it had been a good experience and that he wanted to tell me about it. He was ex-tending grace, and it was a wonderfully redemptive gift that I will never forget.

Over the next three weeks I healed from the surgery, and with each passing day, I was more and more pleased with the results. From the front, I looked as I had always looked. From the side, you could see my nose was smaller, but not enough for most people to notice. In fact, just three weeks after the surgery, I spoke at a large church that uses two huge video screens for services. People looked at my face on giant screens all morning, but if anyone noticed a change, they said nothing. The same was true the next two weeks, when I preached at two more large churches.

The early part of the fall of 2013 was as normal as life can be when you are living at home as a woman and in public as a man. I attended the Orchard Group retreat on the shore of New Jersey and spoke a couple of times to all of the Orchard Group staff. In Novem-ber Cathy and I decided it was time to tell our CEO and his wife what was happening.

I was living parallel lives with contrasting emotions. The male part of me was distraught and filled with anxiety. The female side was thrilled to see the continuing changes taking place in my body because of the surgery and hormones. I loved feeling more and more at peace within myself. I liked the person I saw in the mirror and had no doubt that living as a woman felt more natural than living as a man. The new life that was unfolding made the old life bearable. What happened next shifted that delicate balance.

CHAPTER 11

Eighteen Days in December

When you come out of the storm, you won't be the same
person who walked in. That's what this storm's all about.

—HARUKI MURAKAMI

It was January 2013 and I was in Orlando leading a retreat. Our official day had concluded, and I asked one of my friends if she was up for a serious late-evening conversation. She served on the board of directors of the Orchard Group. My anxiety was extreme. This would be the first time I told someone with whom I worked that I was transgender.

My colleague was young enough to be my daughter. She is intelligent, thoughtful, and good. She listened carefully and responded with surprise but without judgment. Later she told me that after we had finished, she had gone to the hotel bar for a glass of wine. My young colleague was not prepared for what I told her. No one was, which made the telling all the harder.

In April I told another board member. He has a poker face, so you rarely know exactly what he is thinking. When I told him, I knew exactly what he was thinking. Eyes wide with disbelief, he said, "Wait, what? Wait, uh, what?" He stammered for another few seconds before saying, "Well, I didn't see that coming!"

"Yeah, nobody did," I told him. Even though he was shocked, he was also supportive.

I had lived with being transgender for decades, but to everyone else the news was earthshaking. I was an alpha male, the picture of confidence and control, an image carefully calculated over decades of practice. If the first revelation to a board member sent her to the hotel bar, and the second stunned a calm and cool pastor, what could I expect from those who were not going to be supportive? I had chosen these two board members carefully, for the sympathetic ear I expected each would have and for their generosity of spirit.

I told no one else for another six months. Those two conversations were soul sapping. Even though my colleagues were supportive, the look on their faces was enough to cause me to take a break for a while. Throughout those months I knew the most difficult conversation was yet to come. It would be with Brent, my handpicked successor as CEO of the Orchard Group. My therapist friend David kept cautioning me. With great concern he asked, "Are you sure you are not going to get fired? You know, one of those 'clear out your desk and turn in your key' kind of moments?" I assured him there was not a chance I would be treated that way. I still had the confidence that goes with never having been treated unfairly. I believed all would be well.

I made an appointment to meet with Brent on December 12, 2013.

Cathy and I flew to New York the day before, and after taking the grandkids to school that Thursday morning, we got in my old Toyota RAV4, now my son's car, and drove from Carroll Gardens, Brooklyn, to the Upper East Side of Manhattan. Traffic was light, though it took forever to find a parking spot. It was very cold as we walked the last couple of blocks to Brent's apartment.

I had stepped down as CEO two years earlier and moved into the position of nonexecutive chair. Brent was finding his voice, but he still showed a lot of deference to me. I expected him to be gracious enough to allow me to set the narrative of my coming out. Brent and his wife greeted us at the door. After small talk in their living room, I began telling my story. I had prepared Brent, and assumed he had prepared his wife, that they would be receiving information they would find surprising. They had not guessed what it might be. No one ever guessed what it might be. As I told my story, both Brent and his wife responded graciously. I shared my plan for moving forward. I would continue in my current responsibilities as chair for one more year, keeping the information to a small group of board members and staff. Then I would work a second year behind the scenes, letting it be known that I would be leaving at the end of the second year.

I was not prepared to leave the ministry I had led for a quarter of a century and served for thirty-five years. I loved my work. My job as nonexecutive chair was delightful. In addition to chairing the ministry board, I chaired the board of several new churches, helping them make healthy decisions in the first years of their lives. I counseled and mentored pastors, led retreats, and raised funds. I planned to stay in that role until around age seventy. In America, men in their sixties and seventies are seen as still being in their prime. I have learned that the same courtesy is not extended to women in their sixties and seventies.

When it comes to power and influence, men have an advantage over women for their entire lives.

I knew coming out as transgender was going to be a problem for the ministry, and I was sensitive to that reality. The Orchard Group served within the confines of the Independent Christian Churches and Churches of Christ, an evangelical group of around six thousand churches, all of which are decidedly conservative when it comes to LGBTQ+ issues. As a national leader, my coming out would be a shock to the entire denomination. I knew if I tried to remain long-term with the ministry, the Orchard Group would suffer financially, because some churches and individuals would cut off their financial support. But I believed the ministry could grant my request to remain another two years. I had served the organization for thirty-five years. I had kept the information private for an entire lifetime. Surely the board and staff could join me in keeping it private for another two years.

I thought I would be allowed to leave on my own terms whether or not I had decided to transition. Being transgender is not a crime. There had been no moral failure. It is not even mentioned in the Bible. There was no objective way an evangelical could find sin in my circumstances. As we drove back to my son's apartment, Cathy and I talked about how the meeting had gone. I had encouraged Brent to speak with the two board members with whom I had already spoken, as well as a mutual friend I had told eleven months earlier. I thought we could all work together on how to approach the rest of the board.

The next day we flew home to Colorado. Over the weekend I was nervous but not inordinately so. I had already traveled a long pathway. Besides, shortly before we left his apartment, Brent had said, "There has to be a way to work this out." I trusted him.

On Monday, December 16, I did a consultation for a small business in Denver. When I returned home, I had a short and terse email from Brent, informing me that the executive committee of the board of directors had scheduled a mandatory meeting with Cathy and me two days later, Wednesday, December 18, at a location to be determined near the Denver airport. I understood exactly what was happening. The CEO had chosen not to speak with the two board members who had time to think about my revelation. He had spoken instead with members of the executive committee. I felt like a cartoon character getting ready to blow steam out of his ears. I called Brent, as angry as I have ever been. "I thought we had agreed you would talk to the two board members who already had this information. Then together we would decide how to approach the executive committee and the full board."

He told me he had decided otherwise. "Really? Seriously? You've decided otherwise!" I exclaimed. He offered no explanation. I had never been angrier or more hurt. "How cowardly that you didn't give me the dignity and respect of a phone call! How could you communicate such devastating news via email? That is not leadership. That is cowardice!"

He was honest. "I just didn't want to deal with it on the phone," he said.

I told him, "Yeah, well, you're dealing with it now." Cathy was in a graduate class that day. When she got home, I told her about the email and call. She said, "This is not going to end well!"

On Wednesday we arrived at the SpringHill Suites near the Denver International Airport, and Brent escorted us to a room where one of the board members was staying. The other executive committee members had rolled in desk chairs from their own rooms. Cathy and I sat on the couch. Our heads were a good eighteen inches beneath the heads of the rest of the board members. That has always remained with me. Every question came from above. Though I was still presenting as a man, I was already being treated as a woman. Just the revelation that I was transgender caused me to be seen as less than the men in the room. We sat on that couch for over two hours.

I talked about having known I was transgender from as early as I could remember. I told them I fought being transgender and always felt I could keep it private. I shared how I had begun to realize that keeping it private might not be possible. I made it clear I was not committed to transitioning, but was leaning in that direction. I also shared the same plan I had shared with Brent six days earlier. The meeting was difficult and draining but not terrible. In fact, after we finished, we all went across the parking lot to Ruby Tuesday for dinner. I felt good enough that for the first time since Monday evening, I had an appetite. We talked of children and churches and all the things we usually talked about over meals.

While Cathy and I were driving home, she asked how I thought the meeting had gone. I remember my exact words: "I believe they will give me what I am asking for." My stomach was no longer in my throat. I was relieved. When we got home, I went to bed. After a very difficult day, I was exhausted, and slept soundly.

Since the previous October I had been having headaches that came on after five or six hours of sleep. We had done MRIs to rule out serious medical conditions. Only one thing could rid me of the headaches: I had to get up. Within an hour of rising they always went away. But the headaches were coming two or three nights out of every five, and my family doctor referred me to a neurologist. I had an appointment for the morning of December 20.

I woke up that morning with a headache, and grateful for a chance to get to the bottom of the problem. I headed east on Highway 66, a fifteen-minute drive to the doctor's office. As always, I enjoyed driving through the pastureland and gentle foothills before the landscape shifts to endless miles of grassy plains. As I drove through the quaint little town of Hygiene, I got a call from Brent. His voice was tense. He told me the executive committee had decided to recommend to the full board that they terminate my thirty-five-year employment with the ministry, solely because I was transgender. It did not matter whether I transitioned or not. If I was willing to resign immediately, they would provide me with one week of salary for every year I had been with the ministry. If I was not willing to resign and word got out that I was transgender, I would be terminated immediately with no severance.

A thirty-five-year career, more than a third of a century of good work, gone in one tense phone call. I began to dissociate. My next memory is of being in the doctor's examination room, telling the nurse I had just been fired from my job of thirty-five years. She took my blood pressure and, without telling me the reading, said it was "kind of high." I waited a few minutes for the doctor to come in. I told her I wasn't sure I was going to be a very good patient, because I found out I was being fired from my job of thirty-five years for being transgender. Just like that, I spilled it all. I was meeting this doctor for the first time, but she was the available human, and I needed to talk.

The doctor, clearly shocked, said, "That's not legal, is it?" I said, "It is illegal in Colorado, unless you work for a religious corporation, in which case they can do anything they please." She put down her laptop, pulled up her chair, and held my hand. She told me to talk, and I poured my heart out. I have no idea how long I talked. I have only seen that physician twice since that December, but I will never forget her kindness on that awful morning. I left the office and could not remember where I had parked my car in the shopping center where the office was located. I stood outside the door for the longest time before I finally saw the profile of my brown RAV4 in the distance.

I called the vice chair of the board, a man who had been my close friend for over twenty years. I do not remember exactly what I said, but I know I railed, and he listened. He did not defend himself. It was the last time we ever spoke. So many friendships ended that week.

I called my therapist and she said I should come to the office. When I arrived, I almost collapsed on the floor. She took me by the arm and walked me to an armchair where I wrapped up in a blanket and sobbed. She called her husband in her house next door and asked him to bring some hot chocolate. I couldn't speak. How could they do this? I had done nothing wrong. I had not asked to be transgender. I had known these people for decades. You could find people who might not like my theology or personality, but you could not find a soul who would challenge my integrity. Yet I had been fired, just like that.

Later that weekend Brent called to tell me I was to call the rest of the board members and explain to them why I was being let go. If I didn't call them, Brent would. In the two days before Christmas, I had to tell every board member that I was transgender. A fair number were lead pastors of megachurches and were speaking for between three and ten Christmas Eve services that started on the morning of the twenty-third. I made eight calls on December 23 and 24. Each time I began, "Of course, you already know this is an urgent call at the request of the executive committee." That had been communicated in my email requesting a phone call. They had heard nothing from the executive committee or CEO. Then I said, "From the time I was three or four years of age, I knew I was transgender. Being transgender means that you have a distressingly strong conviction you are experiencing life in the wrong body. It is not a paraphilia or sexual-identity issue. It is a gender-identity issue." I worked from a script and spoke without emotion. I spent two days giving Transgender 101 tutorials. A little bit of me died with each call. I was humiliated. No one understood what it means to be transgender. This was not the time to be giving anyone a tutorial. I made the last call at around 2:00 p.m. on Christmas Eve. When I was done, I sat in the oversize chair next to the Christmas tree and stared at the clay pots sitting above the kitchen cabinets. I listened to the ticking of the clock. I felt nothing. I have no recollection of what I did for the rest of Christmas Eve.

Both of my daughters and their families came for dinner on Christmas Day. I played with my granddaughters while the rest of the adults talked quietly. I gave the blessing as we sat down for Christmas dinner. I have no memory of what happened over the next seven days.

My next memory is of New Year's Eve. I was at home, sitting in the living room. I do not remember where Cathy was. I was alone in the same oversize armchair, staring at the same clay pots above the kitchen cabinets, listening to the ticking of the same clock. I wept. I slid to the floor and buried my head in the seat cushion and cried out to God, "Who do you think you are to have made me this way? I am losing everything! It would be better if I had never been born!" I wept until I was spent. Then, lying on the floor with my head still on the seat cushion, I looked at the clock. It was 11:57 p.m. I thought, *In three minutes, for the first time since I was sixteen years old, I will be unemployed.* I also thought, *Right now, at this very minute, forty-one years ago, Cathy and I were pronounced husband and wife.*

CHAPTER 12

The Darkest Night

Most things will be okay eventually, but not everything
will be. Sometimes you'll put up a good fight and lose.
Sometimes you'll hold on really hard and realize there is
no choice but to let go. Acceptance is a small, quiet room.

—CHERYL STRAYED, *TINY BEAUTIFUL THINGS*

I was alone. It was New Year's Day. I had always been afraid my basic constitution had been cracked by some genetic flaw, the one that laid my mother low. I was afraid my worst fears would be realized, that I was weak. Over the next eight months I would discover whether or not I had the character required of a person of courage.

Most of New Year's Day I sat alone in the same oversize chair that had been my refuge the night before. Most of that first week of

January was spent in isolation. I took down the Christmas decorations and thoroughly cleaned the upstairs, as if I could somehow set things right by cleaning. Every time I thought about our financial circumstances, I became frightened.

I had accepted the offer of one week of severance for every year I worked with the ministry. After that I would be on my own, seven years before I intended to be on my own. I became obsessed with making financial projections. I had planned to work with the ministry through age seventy, when a pension would kick in to supplement the money we had saved in our retirement portfolio. I also had two accounts with the ministry that I believed would be transferred to me. Both were restricted funds, designated for my salary.

That first week of January I made a call to see when the funds would be transferred to my account. I was told there was a problem. If they sent the funds, the Internal Revenue Service could view them as excessive compensation and hold the ministry accountable. They also admitted they had a second concern. They were afraid that if their donors found out they had sent the funds, their contributions would dry up. It did not matter that a third of the money was my own money, given to the ministry to defray my salary costs over the next eight years, or that the other two-thirds had been given by another nonprofit organization for the same purpose. Even though both funds were restricted for my salary and my salary only, they were not sure they could forward any of the funds.

I had been working for years with one of the top ministries in the nation that does tax preparation for clergy. I called their CEO and asked his advice. I met with three of their key leaders the very next day, and they explained that they had developed a separate nonprofit ministry to deal with issues related to these specific IRS guidelines. Greatly relieved, I told the Orchard Group about the program, anticipating they would send the funds to that ministry without delay. That was where things stood as I headed to a meeting in Florida the second week of January.

When I got to Orlando, I received a call from my attorney. She said, "We have a problem. Your former employer's attorney said they do not have to give you any of the money that had been designated for your salary." I was livid. When I got home, I called Brent to ask if what the attorney had said was true. Brent could not guarantee that the funds would be transferred and, furthermore, said the ministry would no longer pay into my pension fund, even though the payments were for work done between 1989 and 2011. I would receive the small amount that had accrued, but that was it. I called my attorney and she said, "I don't think they can do that. Was it designated in board minutes that these payments were for work done in the past?" I said yes, it was clear that it was retroactive compensation. She asked for a copy of the board minutes. The next day she called and said the law was murky: "We could fight this in the New York courts, but I'm not sure we would win."

I was terrified, afraid Cathy and I would be penniless and without a way to earn any money. I sat on the couch for hours, staring through the bay window into the dark winter night. Around 9:00 that night I called Laura, my therapist in Colorado, and said, "I need you to call me tonight if you can." When she had not called back by 11:00, I called again and left a message: "I'm not doing well. On a scale of one to ten, I am at a seven. I should be up until midnight or so. If you get this, could you please call me?"

I went into my bedroom and collapsed onto the bed. I was asleep within minutes. At 6:00 a.m. there was a pounding on my front door. I woke in a stupor and looked out the peephole. Two police officers were outside. I opened the door and the first officer said, "Your therapist has been trying to reach you. We think we need to take you to the hospital." I said, "Oh my! I did ask her to call and told her I'd be up until midnight, but I fell asleep after that. I never heard her call." The officer said, "We need you to get dressed and come with us." I said, "I'm a therapist. I understand your concerns, but I am not suicidal. I have zero suicidal ideation." He asked a couple more questions confirming that I was all right, then left. I immediately called Laura. She answered and I said, "You and I need to talk about what a seven is! If I tell you I'm at a nine, then it's time to call the police, but not a seven." I was grateful she had decided to err on the side of safety, but I was embarrassed.

I look back on those days and wonder whether or not I was, in fact, close to ending my life. I suppose it should be alarming enough that I even have to ask myself that question. It was the darkest time I have ever known. A couple of weeks earlier, I had driven home and pulled into the garage and pressed the button to close the garage door, but for a few too many seconds, I left the car running. I thought to myself, *How easy it would be just to leave the car running until I fall asleep.* I turned off the motor and looked through the windshield, and there stood Cathy in the doorway between the laundry room and garage. She said, "I heard the garage door open and close, but I didn't hear the car door close." She knew to be concerned.

I was terrified, exhausted, and embarrassed. How could I not have known the degree to which my life was going to be upended? I had been spending too much time with nonevangelicals to be fully cognizant of how the evangelical world was going to respond to my revelation. If I had been thinking more clearly, I would have known evangelicals would cut me off, even if they were people with whom I had worked for decades. With their offer of a week's severance for every year I had worked, they thought they were being generous. It never occurred to them that there was a world in which a transgender person would never be dismissed from his or her job.

A few days later I spoke with my attorney again, and she expressed her exasperation with the Orchard Group's outside attorney. She asked if I had a back channel to the board. She said, "If you do, now is the time to use it." I called two of the board members, and they committed to helping me. When they tried to find resolution with the board, however, they hit a snag. Other board members were convinced that if I told my tax advisor why I was being let go, his company would no longer be willing to handle my funds. The board members called back and said, "You are going to have to tell the CEO of the tax firm why you were fired." Throughout the entire nightmare of being let go, that might have been the most surreal moment. The board was asking me to confirm that my tax firm would not turn me out as the board had done. I was exasperated. Could this get any more bizarre? It was like I was watching a bad Lifetime movie with an implausible script. Surely they were kidding. They were not kidding.

I called the CEO of the tax firm and asked if we could meet. He told me he was flying home that night and was planning to catch a shuttle to his office. I offered to pick him up at the Denver airport. On the drive to his office, I told him I was transgender. He is a man of few words. He looked over and said, "I don't know why that would change anything." I cried so hard I could barely see through the windshield. The next day I told the Orchard Group that he was aware of my circumstances and was still willing to have the funds transferred to the nonprofit with which his company was affiliated.

I thought we were done, but we were not. The board decided that regardless of the decision of the CEO of the tax firm, they were not willing to give the money to the nonprofit that would hold it for me.

They wanted to send it back to the organization that had donated it for my salary in the first place. The degree to which the majority of these people were working to distance themselves from any decision to place funds in my hands was almost unfathomable. I had worked at the ministry for thirty-five years. I had brought almost all of them onto the board. I preached in their churches and ate dinner with their families. Now they wanted nothing to do with me.

As absurd as the chain of events was, it became even more convoluted. The nonprofit that originally donated the funds was no longer in existence. Graciously, that board decided to put itself back into existence to receive the funds, then send them on to the nonprofit where my tax advisors had established an account. I will be ever grateful for their willingness to help. On March 31, three months after the tug-of-war over the funds had begun, half of the money was finally sent to my account. I could breathe a sigh of relief. The second half arrived three months later.

Those three months before the first check arrived were three of the hardest of my life. I have always worried about money, and now the retirement income I was expecting was disappearing before my eyes. Cathy was still in school, and I knew I would not be able to find work. In fact, my concerns were legitimate. Our cumulative income over the next four years was less than what I earned in my last two months with the Orchard Group. If those additional funds had not arrived, we would have been in trouble.

All but one of the organizations with which I worked fired me as soon as I came out. The last company limited my work upon hearing I was transgender but did honor my contract through its completion, seven months later. In July 2014, I had to make one last trip as Paul. As I prepared to leave, Cathy took one look at me and said, "You are no longer pulling it off as a man. Your body has changed too much."

She was right. I went into the bathroom and looked in the mirror. My face was smooth and my skin was soft to the touch. My frame was shrinking, and my men's clothes hung loosely on my body. My hands and fingers were thin, soft, and smooth. I had already pierced my ears and you could see the piercings on both earlobes. I looked androgynous. As I headed out the door, I was glad it was my last trip as a man.

The trip was only three days long and included telling a co-worker that I had decided to transition. I could see his pain. I loved working with him and realized it might well be the last time we would ever speak. At that point there had been so many losses, you would think one more would have hardly been noticed, but I had worked with Mark for twelve years and I knew I would miss him. I miss him still.

I took my last flight as Paul that night, getting home around midnight. The next day I started sorting through my men's clothes. Some I saved for one of my best friends. Some I gave to a clothing pantry in town. By the end of the day, the only men's clothes remaining were things that held sentimental value.

Two days later, Cathy left on a two-month retreat. She had stayed home to make sure I was all right, but now that the funds had arrived and I was no longer needing to live as Paul, she took a long trip to clear her mind and decide how to move forward. After she left, the house was eerily quiet. There were no sounds coming from downstairs. All I heard was the gentle whoosh of the air-conditioning and the rapid beating of my own heart. For all I had already gone through I had not yet told the world I was transgender. I sat on my patio and prepared a blog post I intended to release the next day. Then I took a self-portrait to include in the post. I slept well and woke up refreshed and confident. I spent an hour tweaking the post and then hit Publish. It was July 29, 2014.

CHAPTER 13

Hope Unfolding

*Learn from every mistake, because every experience,
particularly your mistakes, are there to teach you and
force you into being more of who you are.*

—OPRAH WINFREY

The day I published my coming-out post, there were over six thousand views of my blog. Within a couple of months, that had grown to sixty-five thousand views. I did receive some positive responses, but I got far more angry ones. Most of them had a smug moral superiority. One of the worst came from a former Christian college president. These were people I had known for decades. A week after the initial revelation, I wrote this post:

Here is the truth. I will leave you alone. I will not try to return to your world. You do not have to visit my blog. I think we will both be happier.

But this subject is not going away. People like me are in your church right now. They are struggling and feeling hopeless. Almost half are considering ending their lives. I have heard from them. There are more than you think. They love their church, but few churches are offering them any real hope. They are good people trying hard to be better people. You can pretend they are not there, but most of the developed world has come to realize it is time to let them live in some semblance of peace.

The differences between evangelical and nonevangelical responses was striking. Nonevangelical comments were 99 percent positive. Ninety percent of evangelical comments were negative. I tried not to take it personally. Evangelicals reject others because they are afraid. That a well-known pastor from a conservative denomination could come out as transgender frightened them, and when humans are frightened, they either attack or flee. I was not prepared for the sheer volume of the attacks.

When I came out, I assumed my friends and acquaintances would think, *I guess I don't know enough about what it means to be transgender, because I certainly know Paul's character. I need to study up on this issue.* Surely people would not conclude, *Oh my, I must have been wrong about Paul's character.* But the later is exactly what thousands of evangelicals thought.

When I say I lost thousands of friends, I am not exaggerating. I lost thousands. I have received kind messages from fewer than sixty people from my old denomination. I have heard from hundreds with not-so-kind messages. Every couple of months, when I am traveling through an airport, I see someone from my past. They rarely recognize me. My first instinct is to say, "Hi! It's so good to see you." That is what I want to do. Instead, we pass like ships in the night. I always turn around to see if they turn around. They never do. They just keep walking.

My past does not recognize me. Nor is it ever expecting me. I was at LaGuardia Airport once and saw a family member I had not seen since transitioning. He almost ran into me as he came out of the restroom. He looked me right in the eyes but had no idea who I was. He is a kind man, and I would have gone up to him and talked, but I saw he was with another family member who had written me a mean-spirited letter. I just stood at a distance, one eye peeking from behind a pillar, wishing I could sit down and reminisce. We had a lot of good times together.

Instead, I went back to the American Airlines Admirals Club and talked with one of my friends who works there. I told her what had happened and who I had seen, and she cried with me. I have known her for more than twenty years. But that is my life now. I have received more affirmation and acceptance from American Airlines personnel than I have received from an entire denomination of six thousand churches and two million people. I have been embraced by casual acquaintances I knew as Paul and know again as Paula and have been rejected by those I thought were family. I am a strong person, but even for me, that day at LaGuardia was too much.

In March 2015, Laura, my Colorado therapist, was concerned about my well-being. While I had the support of Cathy, Jael, and Jana, I was otherwise without friends and unemployed. Laura kept asking me to go with her to a PFLAG event in Boulder County, and I kept resisting. She called early the morning of the event and asked, "What are you wearing? And do you want me to pick you up or are you driving yourself?" I relented and said, "All right. I'll meet you there."

About one hundred people gathered to hear the keynote speaker talk about religion and the LGBTQ+ community. Afterward, my therapist introduced me to members of the PFLAG Boulder County board of directors, and I had a long conversation with Jean, the board's president, and Eleanor, another officer. Jean was also the national president of PFLAG. Both Jean and Eleanor are a few years older than me, and they took me under their wing. They introduced me to everyone in Boulder County involved in the fight for LGBTQ+ rights, and Jean went out of her way to connect me to national PFLAG leaders. Because of her influence, that fall I did a workshop at the PFLAG national convention. Eleanor introduced me to fellow instructors at the University of Colorado Boulder, and within a couple of months I was lecturing to full classrooms. Jean and Eleanor and the Boulder County PFLAG team were wonderful to me. Laura had done her work to pull me out of my isolation.

I have always been a Renaissance person, doing a lot of different kinds of jobs. I love being busy. I had many opportunities for meaningful work when I was a man, and I took them for granted. I was a nonprofit CEO, the president of a company that operated homes for individuals with developmental disabilities, an adoption caseworker, a writer and on-air host for a small television network, the editor-at-large of a magazine, and a pastoral counselor. I also started new ventures with friends who were CEOs and, like me, had interests beyond the organizations they directed. We all enjoyed working together and took pleasure in creating companies that improved the lives of others.

We were able to do good work because we all had a head start in life. We all had good jobs in high school and college that others only dreamed about. I was a radio announcer, created a successful band, recorded albums, and spoke to large crowds, all before the age of twenty. My friends had similar backgrounds. We were all sure our successes were because of our hard work, and to some degree, they were. What none of us realized was that we had begun our work lives a lot closer to the finish line than most other people, and miles closer than women and Black and Brown people. I wish I had understood back then just how much of a head start I had been given in life. I may not have been born with a silver spoon in my mouth, but I was born with easy access to spoons.

As a woman, and particularly as a transgender woman, I have had a very different experience. One acquaintance suggested I send a copy of my curriculum vitae to the seminary at which he taught. Shortly before transitioning I had taught a doctor of ministry course that received very high reviews from the students. He said those evaluations, plus my decades in new church development, would go a long way in assuring my resume got a hard look for an adjunct position. I sent him everything he requested, but I never heard a word from the school. When I asked why, he said, "They were uncomfortable with your evangelical background. That plus the fact that you are transgender gave them pause." That last phrase stuck with me. The fact that I was transgender "gave them pause." Over the next three years I had several similar experiences. It was much harder to find opportunities as a woman. I can only imagine how much more difficult it is for a woman of color. That first PFLAG meeting gave me a foothold.

Shortly after attending the PFLAG event, a friend introduced me to Mark, the founding pastor of Highlands Church in Denver. We arranged to meet at a coffee shop, and before our three-hour lunch was over, Mark had invited me to preach at Highlands. I had another foothold. On August 30, 2015, I preached my first sermon as Paula.

The Highlands Communion service takes place immediately after the sermon. As people came forward for Communion, person after person leaned over and embraced me. Their affirmation was life-giving.

Before long I was added to the regular preaching rotation at Highlands. In September, Mark and his co-pastors invited me to accompany them to a meeting of postevangelical churches in Minneapolis. There I met about fifty church leaders from across America who came from evangelical backgrounds but had either willingly left or been expelled from their denominations because they were LGBTQ+ affirming. That inspiring group left me hopeful about the future.

While I was preaching at Highlands, Denver Community Church was working toward becoming an open and affirming congregation, welcoming LGBTQ+ people into its membership. As a part of the process of helping their members understand the change, I was asked to speak on a panel of LGBTQ+ people. Someone from Colorado Public Radio was there, and when I preached at the church later that summer, they asked if they could play the audio of the sermon on their most popular show, *Colorado Matters*. That episode was heard by Helena, one of the curators for TEDxMileHigh, one of the largest TEDx organizations in the world. That is how I ended up speaking for their fall 2017 Wonder event. For the first time since transitioning, I would be speaking to thousands. I was frightened but excited.

In my first meeting with the TEDxMileHigh staff, I was introduced to speaker coaches from the main TED organization. My coach, Briar, is the head of coaching for TED. Briar and I hit it off the first day, when all fourteen speakers gathered to begin two months of intense preparation. Speaking for a TED or TEDx event is wonderful but intimidating. You walk into a room with a very professional staff and carefully curated speakers, and for the first several hours all you can think is, *What am I doing here? They must have been looking for the other Paula Stone Williams—you know, the one who mapped the human genome and ended malaria.* When it's finally your turn to introduce yourself, all you can manage are monosyllables.

When I first talked with the TEDxMileHigh team, no one was sure what subject I should speak about at the event. I suggested talking about why the evangelical church rejects LGBTQ+ people or telling the story of my transition. I spoke with Briar and Helena for hours about the subject for that first talk, and both women kept coming back to the stories I was telling them about the surprises of living as a woman, and particularly the shock of losing my male privilege. They decided that should be the subject of my talk.

Writing that first TEDx talk was transformative. I had to articulate the reality of my male privilege and the fact that I brought some of it with me when I transitioned. But I also had to describe the frustration of losing much of that privilege. As I searched for the right stories to tell, I realized there was no shortage from which to choose. Every week as a female, something happened that reminded me I no longer commanded the respect I once did.

Working on that first TEDxMileHigh talk helped me understand I had a story worth telling. It was the first time I regained some of the confidence that was always present when I was a man. The talk went wonderfully and was rewarded with a long and enthusiastic standing ovation. I was on cloud nine. But I had no idea how much that one talk was going to change my life.

Because of that first talk, Jonathan and I spoke for TEDWomen in 2018, and again for the TEDSummit in 2019. In the fall of 2019, I spoke a second time for TEDxMileHigh. All of my TED Talks have done well online, with millions of views and thousands of comments. But none of them have been as popular as that first talk. Early on I made the mistake of reading some of the comments written in response to that talk. I discovered that unless you are made of steel, it is best not to read the comments. It turns out there are a lot of mean-spirited people out there.

After the first talk I asked a friend to do a little study for me. I asked him to take a look at two hundred comments from each of four different speakers who spoke at that first TEDxMileHigh event. Two of the speakers were men and two were women. All four gave excellent talks. I asked my friend to tally what percentage of comments mentioned the physical appearance of the speaker. Exactly zero of the comments about the men mentioned their appearance. What made that fascinating was that while these men were great speakers, their choice of attire left a little to be desired. On the other hand, my friend said 15 percent of the comments about the women speakers mentioned clothing or appearance. I thought, *Uh-huh, exactly what I thought. Men are judged on the content of their presentation. Women are judged on their looks.* I expected those results, but I was not prepared for one of the observations my friend made. He said that a lot of the negative comments about appearance were from women.

That first TEDxMileHigh talk brought exponential change to my life. I went from speaking on religious and LGBTQ+ issues to speaking on gender equity. I moved from speaking in religious environments to speaking at corporations, conferences, and universities. I had a unique perspective. A once successful, well-educated White man was now a woman becoming frustratingly familiar with misogyny. The challenges of living as a woman were far greater than I had anticipated. When women watched my talk, they were sympathetic, but also a little delighted. Their experience was validated.

Many of the men who watched my talks were clueless and dismissive, rejecting the notion that they had any kind of privilege. There were good guys out there who really wanted to understand, but most of the men who lined up after my talks wanted to tell me how wrong I was. The women at their sides looked at me as if to say, *Do you see what I deal with every day?* I did. As my friend Carla says, women in leadership feel they're carrying the reputations of all other women, to prove women can be trusted and can lead. They are on trial in a way men are not. It is not fair, and as a woman I am realizing just how exhausting it is to be a woman leader. I can only imagine how it must feel when your entire life has been lived under that kind of pressure.

After my first TEDxMileHigh talk, I could see that the trajectory of my life was moving in the right direction. I was grateful for the folks at TEDxMileHigh, for the pastors at Highlands Church and Denver Community Church, for my family, and for my close friends. Now that life was looking up, I could reflect on how difficult the previous four years had been. As I looked back on what I had gone through, I wondered how I had survived.

A few years ago, I was speaking with Gene Robinson, the first gay bishop in the Episcopal Church. We both presented keynote addresses at a religious conference. As we stood at the back of the auditorium, Gene said, "We are strong to go through what we have gone through, and we have found our voice. But I'm telling you, the pain—it accumulates. It accumulates."

The worst of the pain was gone, but its effects had accumulated. I was hopeful about the future but also weary. What kept me going was my conviction that living authentically was sacred and holy and for the greater good.

CHAPTER 14

A New Church and New Life

Doubt kills more dreams than failure ever will.

—SUZY KASSEM

After finishing my work with Highlands Church in Denver, I moved back to my home in September 2017. I was living in our downstairs apartment and Cathy was living upstairs. We were both seeing clients in our home office and Cathy was also working with an inpatient substance abuse treatment program. Outside of the TEDx Talk, most of that fall was spent working with my two co-pastors to get a new congregation, Northern Church,* up and running.

Northern Church held its first services in January 2018. Jessica,

---

* The names of the church and pastors have been changed.

Ryan, and I served as co-pastors, sharing leadership responsibilities. Jessica had befriended me a few months after I transitioned and walked with me through a lot of difficult times. The day we first met she talked about wanting to start a church. Ryan was an entrepreneur who had sold his company and was looking for his next challenge. I talked with him about starting a church-planting ministry. I said, "If you're going to start a church-planting ministry, you need to work in a new church first." The three of us began working together eight months before our first services.

Northern Church began with less than one-tenth of the budget with which we started churches when I was with the Orchard Group. Three postevangelical churches helped fund Northern Church. With a limited budget, we knew we would have to start small and build from there. Within a year we had over one hundred people. Jessica and I shared preaching responsibilities and our different styles seemed to fit the new church well. We added a great music pastor and created worship services we all dearly loved.

I was thrilled to be preaching again. Three years earlier I had thought I would never present another sermon. Evangelical churches shunned me, and mainline Protestant churches were suspicious of my evangelical background. Being added to the regular preaching team at Highlands Church was a wonderful blessing. Being one of the preaching pastors at Northern Church was like winning the lottery.

For me, preaching is life-giving. In a TED Talk I did with my son, I said I believe in God most days, except for Tuesdays and Thursdays and any day I am on the New Jersey Turnpike. The line got a laugh, but it's based in truth. Belief in God has never come easily to me. I definitely do not embrace the evangelical God who looks suspiciously like the earthly leaders of patriarchal religions. To me, God is so far beyond our comprehension that I find it easier to define God as the Big Bang, and Something More. It is the Something More that intrigues me.

I do believe we are made in the image of God, but I have little idea exactly what that means. What I do know is that when I am preaching, I am in love with God. I am smitten by her beauty, in awe of her otherness, and confident of her love. There are times when I finish preaching and think, *Paula, you are not that good.* I'm not saying I am self-critical. I just realize that what I preached was beyond my capabilities. Something holy took place.

And now I was preaching again, and doing it without the harsh bit of evangelicalism in my mouth. Jessica, Ryan, and I were the founding pastors of Northern Church. Jessica was the person whose dream had given birth to the church. She was the people connector. Ryan was the successful entrepreneur, using his skills to help us start a healthy nonprofit corporation. I was the person with the theological degrees and forty years of ministry experience.

Following the example set by Highlands Church, we decided to work without a lead pastor. Was it possible to move away from a hierarchical leadership structure to a flat leadership model? We believed as long as there were clear job descriptions, it was possible. Jessica was the pastor of reconciling ministries, Ryan the pastor of executive ministries, and I was the pastor of preaching and worship. As far as I could tell, through the first eighteen months that leadership structure worked well, and the church grew.

It was the third quarter of our second year that cracks began to appear in the foundation. In a board and staff retreat at my home, Jessica said, "I know we are supposed to be coequal co-pastors, but Paula, your opinion always wins, every time. I do understand that some of the problem is that I need to step up to the plate, but some of it is just that, well, your opinion always wins." The room became

quiet. I held back tears and Jessica awkwardly moved on to the subject we had been discussing. About ten minutes later I couldn't hold
the tears back any longer and went into my bedroom. When I came
back out, I could tell some of the board members were concerned
about me. One came over and gave me a big hug. But when I looked
over at Jessica, it did not look to me like she was happy that I was
being comforted.

I was shocked because, to the best of my knowledge, Jessica had
never told me anything like that before. I did have thirty-five years of
ministry experience in church planting, and I did offer my thoughts
about procedures I thought we should adopt or directions in which
I thought we should move. But I did not think I was being pushy or
demanding. I thought we had been making decisions collaboratively.
After two years of working together, I believed the three co-pastors
had settled into a good rhythm of give-and-take. Jessica felt otherwise.

The next day I asked Jessica for a meeting and we scheduled one
for two days later. As soon as we arrived at the coffee shop, I asked
Jessica what was bothering her. She said, "You are too big for this
church. It's like you're Obama, and we're just this little church in
Longmont." She went on to say if we kept working together, she was
afraid it would end our friendship. I asked her to be more specific.
She said I talked about myself too much, particularly when we were
meeting people for the first time, and that I was always credentialing
myself. She said I didn't need to tell people I'd done TED Talks, or
that I had a movie deal. They didn't really care. Her words stung because I knew they were true.

I have always been insecure. When you have a mother like mine,
it goes with the territory. Now that I am a woman, it's worse. When
I was Paul, I walked into a room and people immediately looked to

me for leadership. My presence was unmistakable, and my credentials were assumed, just because I was a White man. As a woman, I would walk into a room and be resoundingly ignored. People would think I was just an older woman with little to bring to the conversation. I was afraid if I didn't credential myself, I was not going to be taken seriously. The confidence I had as a man was gone. Unfortunately, I could tell some people thought I was bragging when I credentialed myself, and more women thought that than men. Men are accustomed to speaking up for themselves. Women have been taught that it is unbecoming to talk about their own accomplishments, and when they see another woman do it, they are uncomfortable.

How much of Jessica's feelings were because she had been taught that it is not all right to credential yourself, and how much were because it really was unbecoming for me to appear so desperate for attention? It might have been a little of both.

When she said, "It's like you're Obama," I remembered something my therapist in New York had told me years earlier. She said, "Whenever I see Obama walk into a room, he reminds me of you. He walks like you walk." Now that I was a woman, that confident masculine presence was gone. I might bring more presence into a room than some women, but it certainly wasn't like it had been before.

Jessica also said I talked over people, not waiting for them to finish before I talked. I also knew that was true. I had never noticed how often I did that when I was a man, but I was acutely aware of it as a woman. I stopped myself all the time and said, "Oh, I'm sorry. I cut you off." I hated that I did it, but I found it difficult to stop. One of the reasons I hated it so much is because now that I was a woman, it happened to me all the time. It felt like men and women were cutting me off twice as often as they had when I was a man.

Jessica continued to point out my shortcomings and her frustrations, and I did not defend myself at all. I just listened. When I had taken all I could take without breaking down in the middle of the coffee shop, I said, "I think I need to go now."

I got in the car and sat there, staring at the steering wheel. It suddenly occurred to me that I was in the same shopping center I had been in at the doctor's office on the day I had been fired from the Orchard Group. I also realized that though she hadn't used those words, I felt like I had just been fired by Jessica. I drove to one of my best friends' houses and tearfully said, "I'm not sure, but I think I just got fired, though not by someone who has the power to fire me." I wept for hours. Apparently I had let Jessica down in ways I did not even understand.

Most of the accusations were complaints I had never heard before. A couple were things I had heard once before, also post-transition, and also from a woman. They centered on being too strong, though it was never clear exactly what she meant by that. Later, one of the men on our church board asked, "Isn't this the second time this has happened since you transitioned? Did you ever have this problem with women when you were a man?" It was a good question. The answer was no. He said, "I know I'm looking from the outside, but it appears to me that there is a lot more conflict between two competent women than there is between two competent men." His words resonated with me. The truth is that I have experienced more conflict with women in six years as a woman than I experienced with women in sixty years as a man.

Jessica was my best friend and had been there for me when I was going through the worst of times. Now she was telling me she no longer wanted to work with me. She followed up by saying she wanted me to step down as a co-pastor and that she wanted to become the lead pastor of the church. I had thought that might be what the future had in store, but I had also thought it would not happen for at least another year. I wasn't sure she was ready to be the lead pastor. Was that a remnant of my male privilege and worldview, or was it a legitimate concern? I am constantly questioning my own judgment. How much of my perspective is the wisdom of four decades in ministry, and how much is carryover from my days as a male leader in a patriarchal world? The longer I live as a woman, the better I become at discerning the difference between those perspectives. I was fairly sure my concerns were legitimate. She did not have theological training or experience in professional ministry beyond our new church, nor did she have any recent work experience outside of the home. However, I believed she could grow into the job.

I agreed to step down as one of the co-pastors and support her desire to be the sole lead pastor. I was embarrassed. I had no idea she had found me so difficult to work with. How could I have been so blind to what she thought was obvious? When she said she wanted me to step down, Jessica did say it was all right if I wanted to continue preaching for the church. I told her I would like to preach twice a month for at least six months. She thought it should be less.

From that point on, my relationship with Jessica was tenuous. Six weeks later we both presented the plan for her to become the lead pastor, and it was adopted without the board knowing she had requested that I step down. I regret not telling them the whole story. They wanted me to continue to preach regularly, but with the passing of time I realized that was not what Jessica wanted. As we got to the time of transition, it was clear she wanted me to leave completely, though the board did not share her opinion. At her request, I agreed to preach just once a month.

I know if I had still been Paul, I would not have stepped down from my co-pastor role. I did not think the time was right. I would have been confident of my assessment and would have politely said, "Not yet." I would have asked her to be specific about what needed to change, and we would have checked in regularly to assess progress. But now that I was a woman, I did not trust my instincts. If I were still a man, would I have refused to step down because the time really was not right, or would I have refused because of my male entitlement? I wasn't sure. But I was no longer a man. I was a woman who had become aware of male power and entitlement, including my own. I was also aware I had brought my privilege with me. Maybe I had been overpowering. Maybe I was making it difficult for Jessica and for Ryan as well, though he never told me so. It was my first real work crisis as a woman. I had no idea what to do. Part of me wanted to step down just because Jessica wanted me to. But I also knew the rest of the church leaders wanted me to continue to preach. I was miserable.

I had worked in ministry for forty years and built a reputation as a good leader. I had the typical leadership personality you find in most growing organizations. I was an alpha, and at that time, an alpha male. Alphas are natural leaders, comfortable with responsibility. They are willing to go where others are unwilling to go. They are confident, action oriented, and usually successful. They expect high levels of performance from others. Alphas are fast thinkers, which affects the way they do and do not listen to others. They are not always easy to work with. In many environments, the term *alpha* is viewed negatively, skewed toward egocentric, power-grabbing tendencies. Yet in my experience, most alpha leaders are independent, assertive, competitive, courageous, and good leaders.

I arrived in my co-pastor role at Northern Church as an alpha leader, working with two co-pastors who if they had alpha tendencies, they were not as strong as mine. Figuring out the lay of the land was not as easy as I expected. Three years later I can say with confidence that being an alpha woman is nowhere near as easy or straightforward as being an alpha man. I am constantly questioning my own thoughts and actions in ways I never did as a man. Sometimes that is healthy. Often it is not. I trusted my intuition more when I was Paul. I am constantly questioning my intuition now that I am Paula, and there is no good reason for it.

Ryan had always planned to leave at the end of the second year of the church to start a new national church-planting ministry that would plant LGBTQ+ affirming postevangelical churches. When he left in December 2019 and I stepped down from the co-pastor role, we were replaced by two part-time associate pastors who had been members of the church. The two, along with Jessica, now the lead pastor, would lead the church. All three met weekly and carried out the goals approved by the board. I preached once a month, but I was not involved in staff meetings. Jessica became increasingly distraught that I was preaching at all. The board wanted me to keep preaching. I was utterly miserable, not knowing whether to stay or go.

I was deeply upset that my presence was so problematic to Jessica. At the request of the board, I had one final meeting with Jessica in which we were supposed to hammer out a working relationship. It was a cold late-April day in the early days of COVID-19, and we sat on the back deck of the home of the co-chair of our church board. The co-chair was seated between Jessica and me. She asked which one of us wanted to begin, and I asked Jessica if she would speak first. I was nervous but hopeful. I expected her to lay out the parameters for our working relationship. Instead, Jessica confronted me with her frustration that I had refused to step down completely. I asked her to be specific about what I had done since the first of the year that made it difficult for her to lead. Her only response was to say, "What can I say? I am sorry to tell you this, but you are just you." It felt like a punch to my gut. I told her that wasn't particularly helpful, because I was pretty sure I got to be me, and that I needed more details about what I had done wrong. She made it clear that not resigning was what I had done wrong. She felt my continued presence undermined her leadership. I offered to resign and left. It was every bit as devastating a conversation as the one we held at the coffee shop eight months earlier. I had no idea what to do. I sat and stared for hours. Later that day, I realized I did not want to resign without first meeting with the full board, and I emailed the board chair to let her know. I copied Jessica.

The next day, after preaching during the weekly worship service, Jessica told the rest of the staff that she was resigning and had sent a letter of resignation to the board. Shortly after her resignation, the board asked the two new associate pastors to lead the staff on a temporary basis.

It was a very tenuous time for our fledgling church. Many of the leaders were not sure the church would survive. There were a lot of meetings and a lot of tears. At the request of the board, I stayed out of the conversations. After three months of difficult board meetings, the church board asked me to return. The associate pastors were elevated to the position of co-pastor, and the board asked me to also serve as a co-pastor. Another woman was brought on to the team as the fourth co-pastor. I said yes to the arrangement, though not without fear and trepidation.

When we had our first staff meeting, I was nervous. What would stop the new co-pastors from being intimidated by me? Should I allow myself to be me, and let my alpha leadership show? Should I bite my tongue and let them learn on the job without the benefit of the insights I had gained over decades in ministry? I was terrified of doing too much or too little. I was walking on eggshells, fearful of seeing the leadership structure implode again.

To my great relief I realized all three co-pastors were not intimidated by me. They were confident of their own leadership abilities
and respectful of mine. To one degree or another, we were all alpha
leaders. The one male co-pastor is a mergers and acquisitions attorney
accustomed to making decisions quickly. One of the female co-pastors
is a human resources professional who regularly helps employees re-
solve major conflicts. The other woman is an entrepreneur who owns
two companies that she and her co-owner have built from scratch. We
are all independent, competitive, and assertive.

As strong as we all are, it did not take long before I realized that
all three women did not have nearly the confidence our male co-pastor
had. We second-guessed ourselves, worried if we were being too strong,
and didn't want to step on one another's toes. We were also a little wary
of one another. We knew women's tendencies to be critical of other
women. I was intimidated by the other two women and saw myself as
less capable. It required a lot of words for us to work through our wari-
ness and insecurities.

Having been a confident man, I knew exactly what our male
co-pastor must have been thinking: *These women are rock stars. Why
aren't they more confident?* When I talked with him, he said that was
exactly what he was thinking. I explained that in just six short years
I had gone from being a very confident alpha male to a very insecure
alpha female. An insecure alpha female might sound like an oxymo-
ron, but it is not. I know a lot of strong females who are deeply insecure. We are exercising our strong personality traits in a world that is
not always appreciative. After being told that you are difficult to work
with, you begin to believe that you are, in fact, difficult to work with.
When I was Paul, no one said it was hard to work with me. As Paula,
I was being challenged, and it took away my confidence.

I always wondered why women constantly apologize for themselves:

"I'm sorry, guys, but I don't think these numbers add up." I always thought, *You know, you don't have to apologize for being right.* But women do think they have to apologize for correcting the record. They have been told that their entire lives. I have only been told that for six years, but I already have lost much of the confidence I gained through six decades as a man. I don't think it is intrinsic to life as a woman to doubt yourself. I think it is a result of a steady diet of being beaten down simply because you are a woman. The amount of confidence I lost in nine months of conflict at the church was far beyond anything that had ever happened to me as a man. It caused me to question my leadership abilities. It was a terrible time of self-doubt.

All three women who became co-pastors arrived in our jobs with equal parts eagerness and fear. None of us felt secure. Our male co-pastor was the one person who appeared to be confident. Privately, he had his doubts. But like I did when I was a man, he projected confidence to the rest of the world.

All three women co-pastors were tentative and uncertain. As time began healing wounds, we all became more and more comfortable working as a foursome. Our structure was unique, born of the reality that we were all bi-vocational. We were not without conflict, but we learned to communicate with each other. What works for us at Northern Church is not what you see in most settings, but it is working.

I have come full circle to believe that an organizational chart is a good thing, and most of the time there does need to be one chief executive officer. I do not believe hierarchical, vertically based leadership structures are inherently bad. It is when the person at the top gets unbridled power that the organization is in jeopardy. Naming a CEO to an organization is not a problem. The problem is a CEO with unchecked power.

Through the painful process of the church's leadership change, I also came to believe that certain leadership qualities are necessary for a growing organization. The person in charge needs to be visionary, intrinsically motivated, intuitively able to take the right kinds of risks, and have a demonstrated ability to get people to buy into their clearly articulated vision. In other words, I believe organizations are best served if they have a CEO who has an alpha personality. I have also come to believe that on the whole, alpha women are stronger leaders than alpha men.

It was interesting to see the differences between female and male heads of state in the early days of the COVID-19 pandemic. Women heads of state in Finland, Norway, Iceland, Germany, Taiwan, and New Zealand responded far more quickly to contain the virus than male heads of state in Great Britain, Brazil, and the United States, three countries that failed tragically in the early days of the pandemic.

Several differences in the women leaders stood out. First, they were better at showing empathy than the men, making it more likely that their citizens would follow the course they suggested or mandated. Second, the women were more collaborative than the men, engaging their health department leaders as equals rather than subordinates. Third, because they were more collaborative, the women also compromised more easily than the men. They were also much more open to being corrected than their male counterparts. When they realized a plan was not working, they did not double down. They backed up and went in another direction. And finally, the women leaders were better at showing humility than the men. They reminded us that the greatest world leaders have always had equal parts confidence and humility.

With those differences from their male counterparts, these women shut down the first wave of the virus relatively quickly. But make no mistake—they were all alpha leaders, intuitive risk-takers, and excellent decision-makers who had the ability to get their citizens to buy into their vision.

I learned a lot through the turmoil of the third year of Northern Church. I realized that a strong woman leader has a much harder time leading than a strong leader who is a man. She has to fight harder for what she knows is right, but she has to do it without being too forceful. And "too forceful" for a woman has a much lower threshold than "too forceful" for a man. She has to massage the male egos in the room, while remembering that women do not empower one another, so she will have to watch her back. And in the eye of the public, she has to do it all effortlessly.

I am not sure what to think about my own role as a woman leader. I am definitely an alpha leader, and always have been. But there are huge differences between how I express those leadership abilities now as compared to how I expressed them when I was a man. I still find it just as easy to step into leadership. The difference is how it is received. As a woman, I have noticed other women are more inclined to see it as a power grab. The first few times that happened, I was surprised. Though it feels natural to step into leadership, now I am accused of being too strong and too much like a man. In fact, on more than one occasion I have had people say, "Was that Paul who just showed up or Paula?" The first couple of times it happened I was so surprised, I did not respond. When it has happened since then, I say, "Being strong does not mean I am still functioning as Paul. Paula is allowed to be as strong as Paul was." That is usually the last time I hear the comparison.

I feel for alpha females. They are always on a knife-edge. If they are strong, they are seen as "too strong." If they are not strong enough, they are dismissed as not having the leadership skills necessary to qualify for a corner office. A woman is always riding that fine line between being too strong and not strong enough, judged and found lacking by both men and women. It has been one of the most unwelcome realities of life as a woman.

About my relationship with Jessica: She was one of the best friends I have ever had. She helped me figure out what it means to make my way in the world as a woman. She held me when I was in tears because my children were separating themselves from me. She comforted me when Cathy needed to pull away. She encouraged me when I questioned my ability to do my first TEDx Talk. She sat with me when I went through a difficult period of therapy in which I was dealing with hard memories. She was a tremendous support and a wonderful friend. As a pastor she was outgoing, loving, and accepting of everyone. Until those last nine months, I loved working with her. I still do not understand what happened. I am sure we both made mistakes. I know I did. I still believe she is one of the finest people I know.

Every new church seems to have a crisis of some kind during its first few years, and we were no different. You always hope those difficulties make you stronger. I believe Northern Church is stronger, and I look forward to seeing what the future holds.

I love what our church is becoming. Right now, our church has a group studying what the Bible does and does not say about LGBTQ+ issues, another group focused on systemic racism, and another focused on how to be an anti-ableist community. We know the world is broken, but we also know that we get to choose whether to react to its brokenness by running to one extreme or the other, or to react with intentional, extravagant, unconditional love. That is what our team is choosing to do at Northern Church, as we strive to be a light in the midst of so much darkness.

I believe the essence of the Christian message was given by Jesus in his last large gathering in which he took questions from the crowd. When asked which of the 613 laws of the Hebrew scriptures were the most important, he said just three things. He said religion is about loving God, loving our neighbors, and loving ourselves.

In my preaching, over and again I have defined those three commands with very specific language. From the beginning I have taught, "We are to love the God who burst on the scene fourteen billion years ago in all of God's ever-expanding mystery and complexity, rooted in relationship and founded in love. We are to love our neighbor, which is every single human being with whom we come in contact. And we are to love ourselves. If we cannot love ourselves, we will never be able to do the other two." That is the theological foundation of our church.

For me personally, I am finally in the right body, preaching a message I believe with all of my heart, working with people I love and respect, participating in worship services that feed my soul. I have waited my whole life for this kind of spiritual experience. To be able to bring that message to others is one of the highlights of my life as Paula.

CHAPTER 15

Dying before Dying

I am living today as someone I had not yet become
yesterday. And tonight, I'll only borrow pieces of who I
am today. To carry with me tomorrow.

—ANDREA GIBSON

I am constantly reminded how different my life as Paula is from my life as Paul. I transitioned less than ten years ago, yet it feels like it has been decades since I lived as a man. What happened to Paul? Where did he go? What do I do with my memories of him? I have no pictures of Paul on the walls of my home. Not a single one. The occasional piece of junk mail arrives in his name, but it gets dropped unopened in the recycling bin. I have books on my shelves that have Paul's name written on the inside cover, along with the date the book was purchased. They are my books, but that is not my name. I do not know what to do with Paul Stone Williams.

In 2001, I wrote a book of stories entitled *Laughter, Tears and In-Between* that was published by Judson Press, a small religious publishing company. I've kept a few copies for my grandchildren. A few months ago, I was cleaning out the basement and ran across one of the copies. I sat on the floor and read a story or two. Before I knew it, long hours had passed, and I had read the entire book. I wept. I missed the man who wrote the stories. I wanted to have dinner with him and talk about old times. I liked him. Other than being unaware of the full measure of his privilege, he seemed like a good guy, insightful and sensitive, funny and engaging. You could tell he loved his wife, delighted in his children, and did not sail through life unaware.

There were forty-three stories in the book. I was surprised how many made me cry. There was the story about the 1988 Mets game when Jonathan got close to catching a foul ball only to lose it to a brash Brooklynite, and how he redeemed the memory a decade later when he caught a foul ball and gave it to the eleven-year-old kid behind him. And the story about taking Jana to college and hugging her in the stairwell of the girl's dorm as she cried and said, "I can't do this," and I assured her she could. And then driving home and getting stuck behind the ill-placed drawbridge on the Belt Parkway, feeling my entire life had been abruptly stopped in its tracks. What would I do without any of my children sleeping in their beds?

Every story took me to a cherished memory in the life of the man I can no longer find. I remembered crying when I wrote many of the stories, trying to see my computer screen through the tears. I remembered the nature of the things Paul always noticed—the shortness of life, the capriciousness of death, the luck of being born in the United States, the joy of fatherhood, and the security of a good marriage and meaningful work. Paul was grateful for his close friends and wanted to write stories about them so he could memorialize the good fortune that had brought them together.

As I read, I sat on the cool concrete floor with my back against a large box of fall decorations. The box has not been opened since Cathy moved away. She was the holiday decorator. In the fall I put out a pot of mums and call it a season. Just inches behind me were plastic pumpkins and straw scarecrows and all manner of delights that had once reminded my children that Halloween was just around the corner and Thanksgiving, Jana's favorite holiday, was on the way.

Jonathan and Jubi always celebrate Thanksgiving with her family. One recent Thanksgiving, when Jael and Kijana were in New York, Jana had to leave her girls with her former husband before she came to our house for Thanksgiving dinner. Cathy was preparing a traditional meal and Jana arrived a mess. The three of us got into an argument because it was a safe place to pick a fight, I guess, and Jana left within twenty minutes of arriving. Cathy went back to her apartment and I was left with an entire Thanksgiving meal sitting on the kitchen counter. I couldn't bear to look at it and threw every bit of the food in the garbage and watched the sanitation truck carry it away the next morning.

It was one of those days you want to forget but know you never will. Through sheer determination, you refuse to allow it to define your future. But make no mistake, when I went to bed that Thanksgiving night, I was sure if only I could have made it through life without transitioning, none of that would have happened. Jana would be married and her marriage would be fulfilling, Jonathan and Jubi would rotate Thanksgivings between Jubi's family and ours, Jael and Kijana wouldn't feel the family tradition was on their shoulders, Cathy would get out of her warm place next to me in bed to put the turkey in the oven, and all manner of things would be good and right and in their proper place. But here I was sitting on the basement floor with scarecrows in the box at my back, and I didn't know if the scarecrows would ever come back out, and I wept.

How do you grieve a life that is over but still lives on in an uncertain form? Where do you hold your memories of a person you can no longer see, or sometimes even sense? What am I to do with this dying before dying?

In the fall of 2019, my children and I were asked to appear on *Red Table Talk*, Jada Pinkett Smith's talk show on Facebook. We would be interviewed by Jada; her mother, Adrienne; and her daughter, Willow. They were delightful people and we loved being on the show. We did a two-hour taping, which was edited down to a half hour. I was pleased with the final product, but it was not the show itself that had the most lasting effect on me. It was the taping. I was taped for about an hour before they brought Jonathan and Jana on-camera. (Jael chose not to be at the taping, though she had done an on-camera interview in Denver with one of the producers.) That first hour was enjoyable, though it is always emotional talking about the challenges of growing up transgender. It was the second hour that was more difficult, as Jonathan and Jana talked about the discontinuity between their years with their father and their years with Paula. Jonathan still calls me Dad, but the girls call me Paula. We all struggle with how to frame the past. Throughout the taping of the show, that was the theme that prevailed. We talked about the difficulty of knowing what to do with the two halves of our lives.

Shortly after my transition, I kept telling Jonathan I was fundamentally the same person I had always been. I kept saying it because he was the family member who first identified just how different I truly was. Cathy and the girls were seeing me every week. They watched the slow hormonal changes take place, and the way they affected how I navigated through life. They also saw how much happier I was as a woman. I believe that delayed their grieving, which was neither good nor bad; it just was. Because of the time that passed between each visit, when Jonathan saw me, the changes were jarring. When I kept saying I was the same person, Jonathan kept replying, "No, you are not!" The strength of his protests got my attention. It took me a while to realize he was right. The more I see Paul in the rearview mirror, the more I wonder if he, or I, was ever there.

When my mother passed away, I did not feel free to speak at her funeral. Jonathan conducted the service, which brought great comfort, but I would have loved to have eulogized her. But the funeral was in the foothills of eastern Kentucky, a decidedly conservative region, and I knew if I did speak, it would end up being about me, not my mother. I waited and expressed my words about Mom in a blog post I published a week later.

My father passed away in May, six months after my mother, during the early days of the COVID-19 pandemic. I had been able to see him in January, but I did not realize it would be my final visit. I was not able to go to Kentucky when he died or be there for his burial. Because of the pandemic, we were unable to do a funeral service. It was not the way I wanted to say goodbye to my father. I think of him every day. He was such a good man, full of grace and acceptance. I believe the biggest mistake he ever made was marrying my mother. Of course, if he had not married her, I would not be here, nor would my children or grandchildren. The decisions we make have real consequences. I am glad he did marry her. Life is worth living, and I am grateful for all the unseen elements that conspired to place me on this fragile planet.

My mother's funeral and my father's passing made me think

about my own funeral. It is unlikely anyone from my past will be there. It will be a time to celebrate Paula's life, not Paul's. Is that fair? Does it really allow my family to grieve the loss of Paul? It would have been better if we had found some way to memorialize Paul. I wish we had gathered our family sometime shortly after my transition to reminisce about our life together. I wish we had mourned the loss of Paul. We all needed it. I think about doing it now, but it feels like it is too late. Yet it might bring some closure to the first half of our lives and make it easier to celebrate the life we are living today.

There is another reason I am not sure I want to memorialize Paul. Most days, I am not sure I deserve it. As a child, I always had a difficult time feeling I was worthy of love. If we have that feeling in childhood, it tends to remain through adulthood. Whenever Cathy and I watched the movie *It's a Wonderful Life*, she would tell me the world saw me in the same way the townspeople saw George Bailey. The world was a better place because I existed. I had a hard time believing that. I still do. I am acutely aware of my flaws. My mother made sure of that. I always accepted criticism without defending myself. I just listened and took in what the person was saying. I usually waited to talk with Cathy or my therapist before trying to figure out what was true and what was projection or transference.

"Believe the truth will set you free" is not just a phrase; it is a way of life, and it is not easy. I was always committed to knowing the truth, even when it was difficult to hear. I also had a tendency to take in negative words more readily than positive words. The negative words reinforced what I heard in childhood, and we all have a tendency to be more comfortable with adult scenarios that reflect our childhood experiences. It is difficult to grow beyond the story you told yourself when you were a child, and the story I told myself was that I was not worthy of love. There are some wounds we carry with us for life. By every measure, I have been wonderfully loved. I am loved by my children, my grandchildren, Cathy, family members, close friends, and countless others. I was loved by my grandmother, my father, and, in her limited way, my mother. But when you are transgender, and you know you have hurt the people you love, it is difficult to see yourself as lovable. I continue to work at it, because I know I cannot love others well if I cannot love myself well. I am a work in progress, as we all are.

As a woman, I am pretty sure I would have liked Paul. I would have appreciated his gentle confidence, attentiveness, and desire to empower women. I would have become frustrated with how clueless he was to his privilege, but I would have seen him as a man using his power for good. It pains me that in some ways, that man is gone. I try to keep him as a friend, but he is not even accessible in my dreams. I dream about my years as Paul, but I am always Paula in the dreams. I miss Paul. I am allowed to miss Paul without wanting to be him. I do not regret transitioning, but I do miss the man I once was.

I miss my easy way with laughter, and my relationship with Cathy and my children. I miss being a father and husband. I miss being a son and brother. I was a loyal friend who loved nothing more than empowering others. I brought that with me, but I no longer have the kind of power to empower that I had back then. I miss that women knew they could draw close to me without having to worry about me getting the wrong idea. They knew I saw them as an equal, and they appreciated how I carried my maleness. I was not a woman. I was a man.

I liked the clothes I wore. I miss Brooks Brothers shirts and Bills khakis. I miss the physical power I had. I keep separate records of my fastest times as a man and as a woman on running routes. My best times as a man were 10 to 15 percent faster than my best times as a woman. I miss keeping up with Jonathan on hikes in Rocky Mountain National Park and holding my own with him on the narrow single track of a mountain biking trail. More than anything, I miss attending New York Mets baseball games as father and son.

I miss being a father to my daughters. I miss comforting them and giving them the encouragement only a father can provide. I miss being a father figure to others and, as a pastor, being a male representative of God. As a man, my favorite comment I ever received was from a woman who left the church during her college years and had only recently returned. She said, "You make me trust God again."

I know what you are thinking. *Then, for God's sake, why did you transition?* I transitioned because as much as I loved my life as Paul, it was a life of accommodation. I was accommodating what others wanted and needed me to be. I was accommodating a religion I believed in, even though I knew how much it needed to change. I accommodated the wishes of my parents and demands of my evangelical culture. I was trying to please everyone, but it was not from a place of abundance; it was from a place of scarcity. I was scratching for every ounce of energy I could find, trying to be what everyone wanted and needed me to be. But if you believe the truth will set you free, eventually you have to trust the truth. I believed I was supposed to have been born a girl. If I wanted to live authentically, I needed to transition. I truly believe that the call toward authenticity is sacred and holy and for the greater good.

Integrating the two halves of my life is important. When someone calls a transgender woman by her male name, some transgender women refer to it as having been "deadnamed." I do not use that language. Call me Paul, and if it is done with respect, I will still answer. Paul is not my "deadname." It is the name I was given by my parents at the time I was born. It is what Cathy and my friends called me for forty years. I was Paul, and I had a good life as Paul. I do not regret that life. But it was time to transition.

I understand that for many who watch my TED Talks and videos, I am a trailblazer. I am grateful for their words of encouragement, but it's not how I see myself. I am always afraid that what drove my transition was not a call but self-centeredness. I have had a few friends, family members, and co-workers tell me over the years, "Sometimes it's all about you." I have heard it often enough to know there must be some truth to their words. I certainly do not want it to be all about me, but there's not much I can do about the fact that I am me. There are some parts of yourself you just have to tolerate. I caused so much pain to so many I loved. Was it worth it? That is the only truly important question.

Yes, I believe it was worth it. Being at peace in your own body is worth it. Being one with your soul is worth it. Loving others without sacrificing who you are is worth it. As an evangelical, I was taught that love is self-sacrifice. Love is not self-sacrifice. You cannot love well if you sacrifice who you are. Love is extending yourself for the sake of another. It is nurturing your own growth and caring for your own soul so that you might extend love more fully to another.

I do believe Cathy got the best of Paul, but Paula has more to give than Paul. I gave everything I could to our marriage, but it was no longer working. I wish I could have seen a way to continue living as Cathy's husband, but we both realized that was not possible.

My children got the best of Paul, and it was what they needed. That pleases me. I also know that choosing to live authentically and transition was important for my children, though it was incredibly painful for them. One of the most important things a parent can do is live life as fully as possible. That gives their children permission to live their own lives fully. Much of my early desire to excel in the church was to fulfill the unrealized dreams of my parents. It is only when a parent dares to live as fully as possible that their children do not feel the need to live out their parents' unfulfilled dreams. Living authentically is not only a gift to our own soul; it frees the generation behind us to live their best life. My transition allowed my children to make their own difficult choices as they shaped their lives. It gave Jana the courage to end an unfulfilling marriage. It gave Jonathan the courage to step outside our denomination and find his own way as a spiritual leader. It gave Jael the courage to make her way as a teacher, and then as a school administrator.

I have heard bravery described as not being afraid of who you are. Not being afraid of yourself demands paradoxical strengths. You must be at once gracious and unrelenting, accepting and demanding, vulnerable and self-protective. You must be your own prosecution and defense and, ultimately, judge. You must see yourself with a clear but compassionate eye. If all of that sounds hard, it is because it is.

Transitioning strips you of your illusions. You discover those people who were in a relationship with you because you were useful to them, and you watch people flee from you because they do not want to be made uncomfortable. Some cannot bear your attempt at authenticity, because they are unwilling to live authentically. Others truly believe you were wrong, and your transition is an unforgivable sin. You must choose to leave all those people behind. Holding on to them is not good for your soul.

I gravitate toward friends on a similar journey in the relentless pursuit of growth, because they, too, believe the truth sets us free. They make difficult decisions and awaken the next morning with a vulnerability hangover but keep moving forward, because they believe it is the only decent way to live. Their belief in themselves propels them through the desert, unsure of the destination, but certain of true north. Their heart knows the way. I love these friends and family who journey alongside me. I respect the pain they uncover in my life as they uncover pain in their own lives. The truth is empowering, if painful; freeing, if costly; and, as I say time and again, sacred and holy and for the greater good.

Embarking on an authentic journey means you will become acquainted with loneliness. You will have an acute awareness that we all arrive and depart alone. To be sure, there were those waiting on the platform when we arrived, and there will be those waving wistfully as we leave. But we alone decide how we will live in the short time between our arrival and departure.

Paul had many friends and thousands of acquaintances. For most of my life as a man, I did not mind being alone. I found myself to be tolerable, even pleasant, company. I was a public figure, holding down multiple jobs. The precious hours alone were cherished. I was alone, but I was rarely lonely. Since transitioning, I have made the acquaintance of loneliness. I have watched each of my children take their leave for a period of time, a stark reminder that having a close family is not guaranteed. I have watched lifelong friends who tried to stay in touch but found it too hard and slowly took their permanent leave. I have learned what it feels like to wake up to an empty house, morning after morning. I have precious few friends who knew me as Paul. David, my best friend of forty years, is the only friendship that is as close post-transition as it was pre-transition.

Outside of David, Cathy, and occasionally my brother, Myron, I have no one with whom I can talk about old times—no one who remembers playing hide-and-seek in the hayloft, or being nine years old and waving Nixon and Lodge signs as cars drove by, or sneaking into the gym at night to play basketball, or calling my fellow radio announcers on the private phone when they flubbed a word in the news.

The people who share all of those memories act as if I am gone for good, and for most of them, I am.

But here's the thing. I am still here. As sure as an orange sunset lights up the fall sky, I am here on Colorado's Front Range, and I am alive and well.

On the subject of loneliness, I would prefer not to have made its acquaintance. But it does make me grateful for those few fellow travelers and precious souls who know where we are all going on this pause between two great mysteries. They are the ones who love me enough to say, "You know, you can't go back." At journey's end they will be the ones running on the platform to the last inch of pavement, waving and blowing kisses and holding my gaze into the fading light, reminding me that every minute of this precious life is worth it.

PART III

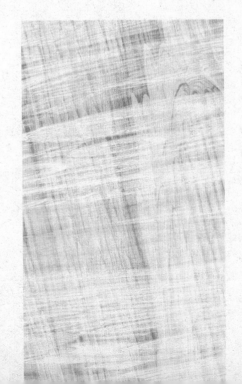

CHAPTER 16

Life Is Easier for Men

Privilege is invisible to those who have it.

—MICHAEL KIMMEL

started flying frequently in 1974, the winter after I graduated from college. I loved everything about travel. Back then, there was a lot to love. Planes were rarely full. Coach service rivaled today's first class. The industry was still regulated by the government, and airlines made money without cramming people into airplanes, charging for checked bags, and extorting high fees to change a ticket. A lot of the airlines were regional, and you felt like you counted. My carrier of choice was Allegheny Airlines, the "Big Airline with the Hometown Touch." In 1982 I purchased a lifetime pass to their airline club for

Cathy and me. It cost $400 total. Nowadays, a one-year membership for one person costs more than that.

Allegheny became USAir and merged with Piedmont Airlines. They were a wonderful airline. When they first created the Chairman's Preferred category for customers who flew over 100,000 miles a year, there were not many of us in the program. I virtually always received free upgrades to first class. USAir, later US Airways, was very supportive of the LGBTQ+ population. Long before marriage equality, they were looking out for their passengers. They later acquired American Airlines, a larger company that also has a good reputation within the queer community.

After I moved to Colorado, I became as close to their employees in Denver as I had been in New York. I met with Karen, one of the Denver employees, ahead of time to tell her I was transitioning. She let my other friends at the airline know, and when I showed up at the Denver airport as Paula in September 2014, they were there to send me off on my first trip. Because I was talking with those employees when we started boarding that day, I didn't get on the plane as quickly as usual. When I did board, there was a newspaper and notebook in my seat, 1D. I usually sit in the first row on the aisle. I picked up the items and put down my laptop, phone, and glasses. A guy about my age was putting his bag in the overhead compartment. When he saw me pick up the items on my seat, he looked over and said, "Lady, that's my stuff." I said, "Okay, but it's in my seat. I'll just hold it for you until you find your seat." He said, "Lady, that *is* my seat." I said, "Actually it's not. It's 1D, my seat." He shot back, "Lady, I don't know what I have to tell you, but that is *my* seat." Again, I said, "Actually, it's not. It's my seat." At which point the guy immediately behind me said, "Lady, could you take your argument elsewhere so I can get on the plane?"

I was stunned. I had never been treated like that as a man. I can tell you exactly what would have happened. I would have said, "Excuse me, but I believe that's my seat." Immediately the guy would have looked at his boarding pass and said, "Oh, I'm sorry." I know because that is what happened all the time! The flight attendant finally took our boarding passes and said, "Sir, you're in 1C; she's in 1D." I put his belongings down on the seat cushion of 1C and he said not a word. Of course, you know who was next to me in 1F. It was Mr. Would-You-Take-Your-Argument-Elsewhere. Karen came onto the plane to give the paperwork to the captain and waved as she left. When I got to Charlotte, I called her. She said, "Paula, what happened? You were as white as a sheet." I told her and Karen said, "Yeah, welcome to the world of women."

It was the first time I was back in Paul's world, doing what Paul had done. Up to that point, every aspect of my life as a woman was very different from my life as a man. This was the first time the two halves of my life merged. Traveling would be a great laboratory to discover the differences between how I had been treated as a man and how I was going to be treated as a woman. As that first trip attested, the differences were going to be significant.

My TED Talks have millions of views and have led to invitations to speak all over the world. Why do people want to hear what I have to say about gender equity? I believe they want to hear from me because I have the unique perspective of having lived life from both sides, and not a day goes by that I am not reminded just how massive those differences are. Life *is* harder for women. I have heard from women all over the world, thanking me for validating their experience.

As I said in my first TEDxMileHigh talk, there is no way a well-educated White man can understand how much the world is tilted in his favor. After I transitioned, I cannot count the number of times I have thought, *I wish I had known this before I transitioned.* There are so many times I have apologized to Cathy for the way I behaved when I was a man. I was always waiting impatiently for her, never understanding why she couldn't be ready to leave the house as quickly as I could. When she had conflict with women co-workers, I assumed she must be lacking conflict-resolution skills. I had no idea how prickly women can be with one another. I got frustrated when she apologized for herself. I had no idea that from the time she was a child, she'd been taught to apologize for herself. I didn't understand why she lacked confidence. She was an intelligent, capable woman. I had no idea women are taught to be perfect, not confident.

Humans are primarily an intuitive species. We don't think rationally as much as we think intuitively. We believe we are behaving rationally, but we usually focus only on the facts that support our position, reinforcing what we already believe. We will take in new information and change our minds, but only if that new information comes to us in a nonthreatening way. Debates are fruitless. They just create more hardening of the categories. We are never going to achieve gender equity by yelling at each other from our respective driveways. We will achieve gender equity when we all sit down together on the front porch and share our stories. It turns out that when it comes to gender equity, my story is unique and useful.

It has been a privilege to come onto the world's front porch and talk about gender equity. I want to validate the experiences of women and help men understand how much the world is tilted in their favor. I certainly did not understand that when I was a guy. As I often say, "I'd better live a long time, because I have a lot to make up for!"

There are countless ways in which I have experienced the differences between living as a man and living as a woman. None are greater than how I experience my sexuality and spirituality. But close behind has been my personal and painful introduction to gender inequity. I experience it every single week.

Last year, I was running in Lihue, Hawaii, and my route took me along the perimeter of the airport. The local media said they were expecting F/A-18s to do touch-and-go maneuvers that afternoon, so a few folks were lined up along the dirt road. I stopped and talked with a couple who had a beautiful parrot with them, perched on the husband's shoulder. They said the parrot liked airplanes. Okay. We watched several commercial airliners land. At one point, the wife commented, "I think that's one of the new Hawaiian Airlines Airbus planes coming in." I took a look and said, "No, I'm pretty sure that's not an A321. It's a United 757, coming from Denver or San Francisco." The woman asked, "Oh, are you a flight attendant?" I answered, "No, I just know way too much about commercial airliners." It was the first time I had ever been asked if I was a flight attendant. When I was still living as Paul, people would ask, "Oh, are you a pilot?" Not now. The conventional narrative is that men are pilots, so a woman must be a flight attendant. Stories like that happen frequently. A lot of them relate to the travel experience, because that is the part of my current life that most resembles my previous life.

You may or may not be aware of this, but many hotels do not really allow you to control the temperature in your room. There is a thermostat on the wall and you can put it on a specific number, but unlike the thermostat at your home, the number does not mean what you think it means, that the HVAC will hold the desired temperature. The hotel thermostat is programmed to stop you from getting the exact temperature you want. It is set to save energy. Many hotels have a system we frequent travelers have figured out how to disable. After you have overridden the program, the screen reads "VIP," which means movie stars, should they stay at your hotel, would not have the same experience you have. Yeah, I know. This is not a fair world.

I was in a Marriott property that had a temperature control mechanism I have come to dread. If there is an override, I don't know how to activate it. I set the temperature at seventy, but the heater did not kick off until seventy-three. Then the room got progressively colder until the heater finally kicked back on at sixty-seven degrees. I called engineering and prepared for the misogyny that was coming. A young man of about twenty-five knocked on the door. I answered and said, "There is a problem with the heating unit, and I would like for you to listen until I have explained the problem to you." I tried to tell him that I knew there was a governor on the heating unit but that a six-degree swing seemed extreme, and I wondered if he could override the governor. He said, "There's no governor on the unit."

I said, "I am a lifetime Titanium member. I have been staying in Marriott properties since before you were born! Don't tell me there is no governor on the unit." He continued to mansplain until I said a third time, "You are not listening to me. I know there is a six-degree temperature swing programmed into the thermostat. I just want to know if you will override it or not." He kept on talking. I was furious. I opened up my computer and pulled up a picture from my first TEDxMileHigh talk and asked, "Do you know what this is? This is a picture of me speaking to five thousand people about how women are not treated with respect. And yes, as you can see, I got a standing ovation. Do you know why I got a standing ovation? Because women are sick and tired of being treated as if we don't know what we are talking about."

I continued my lecture. "Now, here is what is going to happen. The next time I speak to five thousand people, I am going to tell them about you, and your hotel, which I will call by name. And I have a feeling your general manager is not going to be very happy about that!"

I was exasperated. It is also possible that I might have cursed a little. The young engineer left, and much to my surprise returned a half hour later and sincerely apologized. He said, "I was raised by a single mom, and if my mother knew I treated you like that, she would be furious." He then proceeded to program the thermostat so it would hold the exact temperature I wanted. I told him I respected the courage and character it took to admit his mistake. Truth be told, I felt kind of tender toward the guy. I had been pretty tough on him.

Being ignored and questioned is one of the most maddening aspects of being a female. The misogyny is routine. I have stayed in Marriott hotels for four decades. When things like that happen—and they happen far too often—I want to yell, "I know what I know, dammit! Listen to me!"

I would love to say that when I was a man, I was never guilty of mansplaining. But I would be lying. Not long ago, when I was talking with Cathy about a connectivity problem she was having with the Internet, I said, "You need to do this and that." *You need* and *you should* are still in my vocabulary. I caught myself and apologized, but mansplaining does not die easily. Maybe some of my experiences are just the old adage coming true: "What goes around comes around."

I do believe there is one way in which men can identify their own mansplaining. As soon as you are planning to say, "You need to" or "You should," you can be certain that what you are going to say next will be spoken with some level of condescension. I do understand that a tendency to mansplain is related to the differences between the sexes. When men talk about a problem, they are usually looking for answers. When women talk about a problem, they sometimes

just want to talk about the problem. They are not necessarily looking for answers. A man who jumps in to "help" is not what a woman
wants or needs. Unfortunately, the man does not know that. Guys
would be well-advised to wait until a woman specifically asks for
help. Even then, it is best to avoid using phrases like *you need* and *you
should*.

I have discovered that as a woman, I am not judged on the aggregate body of my work. I am judged only on my most recent accom-
plishment, or on the one narrow area of expertise that credentials me
in the eyes of the other people in the room. I was on the board of a
corporation that had a new CEO we wanted to have speak for a large
conference. We talked about having her give a keynote address, and I
suggested that since she was not a seasoned public speaker, we could
interview her instead. I said, "But if you want her to give a keynote,
I'd be glad to coach her." At which point a rather powerful White
man in the room said, "Well, if we are going to do that, why don't
we hire a *real* coach." I said not a word, waiting for someone to come
to my defense. No one did. I stewed and thought to myself, *And why
would I not be considered a real coach? I have taught public speaking at
universities and seminaries. I have done four TED Talks. I have spoken to
crowds of thousands all over the world. I have even coached TEDx speakers and served as a TED Speaker's Ambassador. What part of that is not a
"real" coach?*

I was brought onto that particular board because I used to teach
a graduate course entitled Current Trends in American Religion.
Most of my career has been spent in ministry, studying the American religious landscape. The board knew that, and from at least this
one man's perspective, it was apparently the only reason I had been
brought onto the board. It was not conceivable that I might have addi-

tional gifts, like public speaking, or coaching speakers. As a woman, surely I was not credentialed in multiple areas.

After he made the comment about hiring a "real coach," I never did speak up, because that is another thing I have discovered as a woman: You are always on a knife-edge. If you speak too boldly, you are a threat to the men in the room. If you do not speak up, no one will see you as a leader. No matter what you do, it is wrong. And even if you do speak up, you are likely to be interrupted, because men interrupt women twice as often as they interrupt other men. And it is not just men who are guilty of interrupting women. Women also interrupt women more than they interrupt men.[*]

Men talk more in business meetings than women do.[†] Men are encouraged to think out loud in a meeting. Boys are taught to be confident. Girls are taught to be perfect. Boys will speak up and hold the floor until an idea comes to them. Women do just the opposite. They plan their words carefully, knowing they must speak quickly and succinctly. Women are more formal and prepared, because they have to be.[‡] Knowing they will be interrupted, they have to find the perfect words before they speak. Because they are holding back, someone else speaks up and beats them to the punch.

My gender and age used to give me an advantage. As soon as I stepped into a meeting, there was a predisposition to see me as powerful and capable. That's the way it is in a patriarchal White society. Older executives are revered, and no White men have to leave a part

---

[*] Adrienne B. Hancock and Benjamin A. Rubin, "Influence of Communication Partner's Gender on Language," *Journal of Language and Social Psychology* 34, no. 1 (May 11, 2014).

[†] Marianne LaFrance, "Gender and Interruptions: Individual Infraction or Violation of the Social Order?," *Psychology of Women Quarterly* 16, no. 4 (December 1992).

[‡] Kathryn Heath, Jill Flynn, and Mary Davis Holt, "Women, Find Your Voice," *Harvard Business Review*, June 2014.

of themselves at the door. The meeting was designed for them. They get to bring all of themselves into the room. And it is not just in the boardroom. It is everywhere. Most environments show more respect toward men than they show toward women. And sometimes, women are as guilty of showing a preference for men as men are.

A few years ago, I was flying from Los Angeles to Honolulu on an Airbus A321, a plane not really designed for that kind of trip. The older versions of the plane barely have the range to even make the trip. As we flew through bad weather, the flight became extremely bumpy. The woman seated next to me was quite frightened and looked over and said, "This is scary. I don't understand why it is so bumpy." I said, "Well, we're on an A321, and it's a little underpowered, so until the pilot burns off some fuel, he won't be able to get up above the weather." The woman looked at me like I had three heads. A few minutes later a male flight attendant came by and she asked, "Why is it so bumpy?" He turned back and dismissively answered, "Because we can't fly above the weather yet." She said, "Oh, thank you." I thought, *Wait a minute! I just told you why we can't fly above the weather yet and you looked at me like I had three heads*. But I didn't say anything, because that is my new life. My gender causes some people to believe there is no way I could actually know something, and particularly something about a male-dominated field like aviation.

My gender is only half the problem. My age also works against me. When I was a man, my gray hair and stature inspired confidence in what I was saying. Now most people assume I am an older woman whose better days are over. They do not even look at me, let alone listen to me. I no longer command a room when I walk through the door. I am ignored. I have forty years of experience in church planting. I even wrote two books on the subject. Yet when I am in a church-planting meeting, people ask, "Who are the experts we can turn to?"

Sometimes people point to me and say, "She literally wrote the book. Why don't we ask her?" But with one or two notable exceptions, that's not the way it normally plays out. It is assumed I do not have the same level of expertise as a man. After being treated that way often enough, it creates a deeper problem. The more it is assumed I do not know what I am talking about, the more I begin to question whether or not I do, in fact, know what I am talking about! I understand a woman's tendency to doubt herself.

Did you ever notice that when a woman knows she's right, she apologizes for it? "I'm sorry, guys, but these numbers don't add up." You know, you don't have to apologize for being right! I was working with two ministers from a Unitarian Universalist Fellowship and we were talking about time management. One of them said, "Well, we could accomplish all of these objectives if we didn't spend an hour a day apologizing." She is on to something.

A woman's work experience is vastly different from a man's experience. The most recent annual study, *The Simple Truth about the Gender Pay Gap*, indicated that on average White women earn 82 percent of what their male co-workers earn. Black and Brown women earn even less. Only four states have pay equity for women: Massachusetts, Illinois, Oregon, and North Dakota.

In the American church, women earn 75 percent of what men in comparable positions earn. But that does not tell the entire story. The top four positions in an evangelical church—lead pastor, teaching pastor, executive pastor, and worship pastor—are positions not generally available to women. Of the one hundred largest churches in the United States, not a single one has a lead pastor who is a female.

A study published by the Annenberg School of USC said 28.1 percent of characters in one recent year's top one hundred films were female and only 21 percent had a female lead or co-lead. Less than

2 percent of the directors were women, as were 11.2 percent of the writers and 18.9 percent of the producers. Women lag far behind men in almost every area of the entertainment industry.

Seventeen percent of the biographies on Wikipedia are of women. Could that be because the vast majority of Wikipedia curators are White males? In 2017, 4.8 percent of Fortune 500 CEOs were female, as were 22 percent of senior vice presidents. Women make up 47 percent of first- and second-year law firm associates, but only 15 percent make partner. In the world of technology, women constitute just 22 percent of software engineers and 6.6 percent of chief executives. Less than three percent of venture capital goes to female-founded firms.

I become angry when I realize I am being paid less as a woman for the exact same work I used to do as a man. The myth is that women don't get raises because they don't ask for them. The truth is that they ask for them every bit as often as men. They just don't get them. At the rate we are going, it will be one hundred years before we have pay equity in the United States, let alone any other kind of equity.

My female life has been a sober awakening. We live in a world tilted in favor of White men, and until that changes, gender equity is just a dream. If I knew in the early days after transitioning what I know today, what might I have done differently? A lot!

On that very first flight I would have immediately asked the flight attendant for help. I would have assumed, correctly, that a man was not going to take my word for which seat was mine. It still happens, and that is what I always do.

At the hotel with the temperature problem, when the engineer came to the door, I would have immediately and directly asked, "Would you please override the thermostat so I can set an exact temperature?" If he had claimed ignorance that an override existed, I would have called his manager on the spot, while he was still in the room. Life is too short for long, stressful interactions.

What about apologizing when you know you are right? At my first TEDx Talk I said, "You know, you don't have to apologize for being right." But here's the thing. I've discovered that some male egos are more fragile than others. If I am dealing with one of those fragile egos, it is easier to couch my correction in a quick, "I'm sorry, but . . ." Is that feeding the patriarchy? I suppose it might be, but it's just a tiny morsel, and you only have so much energy.

To me there is nothing more maddening than being interrupted when I speak. I have decided that is one place I will take a stand. The first time I am interrupted, I let it go. The second time, I say, "Excuse me, I haven't finished yet." That usually takes care of it. If another woman is interrupted, I immediately interrupt the interrupter and say, "Excuse me, but I don't believe she was finished yet." I wish more women would do that. It takes the person who has been interrupted off the hook and is very effective at putting men on notice. The truth is that a lot of men do not realize they are interrupting, and when it is brought to their attention, they apologize. And yes, I do remember writing earlier in this book that I am still guilty of interrupting and talking over others. As I said, I'm working on it.

It will take a lifetime to adjust to the fact that the world is no longer tilted in my favor. And I am fully aware that in many ways, the world still benefits me. Yes, I am a woman, but I am White, well educated, and a professional. When I transitioned, I brought a lot of privilege with me. The world still treats me far better than it treats most women. I do not take that for granted. It is also what motivates me to use every bit of privilege I have to fight for gender equity.

I do not want to close this chapter without dealing with one prickly subject. While so much of gender inequity has been imposed

on women from the patriarchy, there is one area in which women create their own inequity. One of the biggest surprises of being a woman
is learning how much women do not empower one another.

Now that I am a woman, I have discovered how tough women
can be on one another. Men empower one another. When men come
into a room, the first thing they do is determine who the alpha personality is in the room; then they rank themselves according to the
alpha. With rank established, the men get about the business of advancing the agenda of the alpha. Or to use an American sports anal-
ogy, men get in a huddle, smack each other on the butt, and advance
the quarterback and ball down the field. As long as they know their
place in the food chain, men empower other men. Women do not
empower one another.

I believe one of the reasons is that so few women get to leadership positions that when they do finally move into a corner office, they
think, *I worked hard to get here. Why should I make it easier for you?*
Part of the problem is that women have been taught to defer to others, particularly White men. A woman works hard to hold back her
natural leadership abilities. She has been taught that it is not all right
to be an alpha woman. Resentment builds, but despite the obstacles,
she manages to rise through the corporate ranks. When she sees another woman with equal or lesser abilities who feels strong enough to
take the reins of leadership, the woman thinks, *Wait a minute! I've been
biding my time for years, waiting for a shot at leadership. And you come
in here thinking you can take the reins of leadership that might have been
mine? Oh no, I don't think so.* That kind of thinking is understandable.
Competition for lead spots is harder for women than it is for men.

I believe there is another explanation for why women do not empower one another. Men are raised to be confident, while women are
raised to be perfect. A new position opens up in the company that

has five requirements. A man has two of the five and thinks, *I've got this*. He has been taught to be confident. A woman looks at the five requirements and thinks, *I only have four of the five. I can't apply for that position*. The woman thinks that way because she was taught to be perfect, not confident. Even if a woman ends up getting the position, she is not as confident as a man might be, which might cause her to question her own leadership abilities so much that she is threatened by other women who come alongside her.

In my own experience, I have seen women in leadership who are resentful of younger women having an easier time than they had. I have also observed women who are insecure in their own leadership and are therefore threatened by another woman in close proximity. But mostly I have seen women who are so angry about the patriarchy that they have come to reject all hierarchical systems, which causes them to negatively evaluate women with strong alpha personalities. They believe those women have sold their souls to the patriarchy.

It is unfortunate, because strong alpha women should not be punished because they have the ability to work within hierarchical systems. They should be celebrated. It has been my experience that most strong alpha women create healthy collaborative environments that make their organizations successful.

I want to be a woman who empowers other women. I brought my privilege with me when I transitioned, and I want to use that privilege wisely. We all have abilities, gifts, and pinnacle gifts. An ability is something you are able to do but you do not necessarily enjoy. A gift is something you enjoy so much you lose track of time when you are doing it. A pinnacle gift is a gift recognized by others to be extraordinary. In my experience, not many women know where their gifts lie, let alone their pinnacle gifts. They have never received the steady stream of encouragement a man receives.

I want women to know the areas in which they are gifted. I want them to understand that they have abilities that, once identified, accepted, and nurtured, can cause them to soar. I want women to know that when they are in their sweet spot, they are unstoppable. And I want to do everything I can to help women find their pinnacle gifts. The world needs what women have to offer, and the sooner women believe that important truth, the better off we all will be.

CHAPTER 17

What I Wish I Could Tell Paul

It is by standing up for the rights of girls and women that
we truly measure up men.

—DESMOND TUTU

I'm usually pretty hard on myself when I talk about my years as a man, particularly when it comes to gender equity. I can also be hard on myself as a woman. I lived decades as a man and brought a lot of male privilege with me. Whenever my behavior reflects that entitlement, I am reminded that, to some degree, I will always live in the borderlands between genders. I take that humble instruction as motivation to work toward gender equity, and nowhere is gender inequity more of a problem than in conservative religion.

Within my old denomination, I wonder if gender equity will ever arrive. I'm not sure why women stay in the evangelical world. I was a champion of women preaching and also wanted to see the day arrive in which we could hire a woman to be the lead pastor of a new church. Unfortunately, if we wanted to keep our existing income, that was a distant goal. I thought it was all right to wait a few more years. It was not.

There are not many places in Western culture in which women are more marginalized than in conservative religion. If I could go back and speak to Paul, the first thing I would say is, "Hire women as lead pastors and take the financial hit. If you have to downsize the organization, then downsize the organization. But do the right thing." What additional advice would I give Paul?

My 2019 TEDx Talk was targeted to men. When I look at the footage of that video, you see a lot of men with their arms crossed. I don't think that is a good sign. When I was working on the talk, my TED coaches said, "The goal is to get women to watch this video, and then ask their husbands to watch it. The men are not likely to watch it on their own." Has that happened? As of this writing, it's had several hundred thousand views, so at least some people have found it helpful. One of my friends checked out the comments and found a lot were from people asking whether the talk was about male privilege or class privilege. Men like to shift the blame. "She's talking about white-collar privileged men, not blue-collar men like me." I suppose they have a point. I did have more privilege than most. But I think they miss the larger point. All men, including the ones who think they grew up without privilege, have more privilege than the women in their respective worlds.

If men would listen, what would I tell them? In my meetings with white-collar men, the first request I have is basic: "Please, invite us to the meeting." Before I transitioned, I was in a meeting of the executive committee of the national convention of my denomination. When I looked around the room, I realized not a single woman was on the committee. I said, "Guys, this is the twenty-first century. Don't you think we are a little late bringing women onto the executive committee?" One of the more strident males, the lead pastor of one of the largest churches in America, said without irony, "But that would change the tone of the meeting." I looked around to see if shock was registering on anyone else's face. Nope. Not a man was surprised. Equally disturbing was that I dropped the subject. I had done my part, right? Hindsight can be so self-indicting.

How many decisions are made during dinner at a restaurant, after the women on the team have gone home to their other full-time job—taking care of their family? How many are made on the golf course, or at the baseball game? This is one of the most inappropriate realities of corporate life. Men make major decisions after hours, in informal meetings closed to most women. It is all right to make decisions out of the office, but not unless every woman is able to be present.

I used to go hiking in Rocky Mountain National Park with the senior leadership team of the Orchard Group. We would stay together in a cabin, hike or snowshoe all day, then spend the evening enjoying a good meal and talking about life. Humans think more creatively when they are moving, so we did a lot of shoptalk on the trail. There are two problems with those trips. The first is that we had no women on our senior leadership team. And even if we would have had women, they would not have been on the trip, because duties at home keep women from staff retreats more often than they keep men from retreats. Unless everyone can be there, the golf course, tennis court, basketball court, and hiking trail are not where anyone should be conducting business.

Unfortunately, the off-campus meetings are only part of the problem. I am surprised at how often women are not invited to a meeting at the office. I have been left out of more meetings in six years as a woman than I was in four decades as a man. I can't believe how often I have heard someone say to me in a questioning way, "Wait, you weren't in that meeting. Why weren't you there?" Uh, huh. Why wasn't I there? I wasn't there because I didn't even know about the meeting. First, make sure women are invited to the meeting.

Second, do not think having a few women on your work team is enough. Women are over half of the workforce. Your work environment should reflect that. The more female leaders there are, the more supported both junior- and senior-level women feel.[*] Women usually want to work collaboratively. Respect that innate, female preference.[†] Make sure meetings are broken into unranked smaller discussions, and if you are leading the meeting, make sure you interact one-on-one with every person in the room. That will not only make the women on the team feel valued, but it will also make all the introverts happier. When a meeting is broken down into smaller groups, everyone gets a chance to speak.

Make sure women receive credit for their ideas. Women are less likely to have their ideas correctly attributed to them.[‡] A man will give another man credit for his ideas, even if that man is beneath him on the organizational chart. A man is less inclined to credit a woman for her idea, even if she is equal to him on the chart. I was once in-

---

[*] Joan C. Williams and Rachel Dempsey, *What Works for Women at Work: Four Patterns Working Women Need to Know* (New York: NYU Press, 2014).

[†] Jonathan Haidt, *The Righteous Mind: Why Good People Are Divided by Politics and Religion* (New York: Vintage Books, 2013), 178.

[‡] Madeline E. Heilman and Michelle C. Haynes, "No Credit Where Credit Is Due: Attributional Rationalization of Women's Success in Male-Female Teams," *Journal of Applied Psychology* 90, no. 5 (September 2005).

volved with a small corporation on the West Coast in which almost all of the employees were women, but the CEO was a man. On several occasions I saw him claim the women's ideas as his own. The first time it happened, I saw one of the women rolling her eyes at another woman in the room. I asked later what was going on. She said, "We roll our eyes a lot around here. We bring an idea to the table and it doesn't take more than an hour for history to be rewritten. We just laugh it off. What else can we do?" What makes it more ironic is that this boss is quite a public champion of women.

Jocelyn Bell Burnell was an astrophysicist who co-discovered radio pulsars in 1967. When the discovery was recognized with the Nobel Prize for physics in 1974, she was not one of the recipients of the prize, though she had been the first to observe the pulsars. In 2018 she was finally recognized for her work and was awarded the Special Breakthrough Prize in Fundamental Physics. She decided to devote the $3 million she received to scholarships for female, minority, and refugee students who want to become physics researchers. Her story is a reminder to everyone. Make sure women receive credit for their work.

It would be helpful if men understood how effective women are in the workplace. Women are more collaborative[*] than men. They are more profitable,[†] more inclusive,[‡] more effective leaders,[§] less likely to take *unnecessary* risks,[¶] and excellent at multitasking,[**] and they have

---

[*] "Managing Unconscious Bias," Facebook, accessed November 1, 2020, http://managingbias.fb.com.

[†] *Strategic Management Journal* 33, no. 9 (September 2012); *American Sociological Review* 74, no. 2 (April 2009).

[‡] *Human Relations* 69, no. 7 (February 2016).

[§] *Journal of Applied Psychology* 99, no. 6 (January 2013).

[¶] *Quarterly Journal of Economics* 116, no. 1 (February 2001).

[**] Katty Kay and Claire Shipman, *The Confidence Code* (New York: HarperCollins, 2014).

a higher emotional quotient than men.* True gender equity across the corporate world would increase US GDP by 26 percent.†

I do not understand why men do not hire and promote mothers. Women job applicants with children at home are 44 percent less likely to be hired for a job than childless women with similar qualifications.‡ Yet they are extremely efficient workers, great multitaskers, and better at assessing risks than other employees. All that, plus they bring snacks! What more could you ask?

One of the biggest problems for working mothers is that only a minority of companies endorse flextime or working from home, even though studies show that mothers working from home are every bit as efficient as employees who work in the office. Unfortunately, companies act like we still live in the 1950s, where there is one full-time breadwinner of the household, a male, and one full-time homemaker, a female. That was not even true in the '50s. It certainly is not true today. Do not assume mothers are not dedicated to their jobs. Instead, assume your systems are outdated. Most corporate systems are designed for a world that no longer exists. Women are more than half of the American workforce. The systems need to change, not the mothers. Hopefully after the COVID-19 pandemic has ended, companies will realize productivity was not harmed when employees worked from home, and working from home will become a long-term option.

---

* *Journal of Applied Psychology* 95, no. 1 (January 2010).
† Jonathan Woetzel, Anu Madgavkar, Kweilin Ellingrud, Eric Labaye, Sandrine Devillard, Eric Kutcher, James Manyika, Richard Dobbs, and Mekala Krishnan, "How Advancing Women's Equality Can Add $12 Trillion to Global Growth," McKinsey Global Institute, September 1, 2015, https://www.mckinsey.com/featured-insights/employment-and-growth/how-advancing-womens-equality-can-add-12-trillion-to-global-growth#.
‡ Shelley J. Correll, Stephen Benard, and In Paik, "Getting a Job: Is There a Motherhood Penalty?," *American Journal of Sociology* 112, no. 5 (March 2007).

Another problem is that men reinforce stereotypes about women's emotionality. There is no evidence that women are more emotional at work than men.[*] In fact, the evidence shows the opposite. Men are more emotional. Unfortunately, the primary emotion shown by men is anger. Expressing anger is more tolerated from men that it is from women. Angry women are seen as "unhinged" or "unbalanced." Regardless of your gender, it is all right to be angry.

One of the biggest problems faced by men is their inability to see their own implicit bias. According to a New York University study, a man who stays late at work is evaluated 14 percent more favorably than a woman who does so. Yet when neither stays late, the woman is docked for it, given a 12 percent lower rating, while a man is not. Women's mistakes are noticed more and remembered longer.[†] Black and Brown women are even more negatively evaluated.[‡]

Because of these disparities, women are twice as likely to feel burnout as men,[§] in part because men get five more hours of leisure time a week than women.[¶] Women also experience burnout more often because they have to prove their competence over and over. They are not judged on the aggregate body of their work but only their most recent offering. When I was a man, I did not feel like I

---

[*] Williams and Dempsey, *What Works for Women at Work*.

[†] Sara Rimer, "Social Expectations Pressuring Women at Duke, Study Finds," *New York Times*, September 24, 2003.

[‡] Ashleigh Shelby Rosette and Robert W. Livingston, "Failure Is Not an Option for Black Women: Effects of Organizational Performance on Leaders with Single versus Dual-Subordinate Identities," *Journal of Experimental Social Psychology* 48, no. 5 (September 2012).

[§] National Health Interview Survey, Centers for Disease Control and Prevention, 2010/2011.

[¶] Bruce Drake, "Another Gender Gap: Men Spend More Time in Leisure Activities," Pew Research Center, June 10, 2013, https://www.pewresearch.org/fact-tank/2013/06/10/another-gender-gap-men-spend-more-time-in-leisure-activities/.

needed to come into a meeting with a copy of my curriculum vitae. Everyone knew I had competence in multiple disciplines, and they treated me accordingly. A woman is only remembered for her most recent work, and just like my experience with the corporate board, she will only be seen as competent in one narrow area. No wonder women experience burnout twice as often as men. They are over half the workforce, working just as hard as men, but they have far fewer opportunities for advancement. That is a recipe for burnout. Opportunity to practice one's skills, to be appropriately recognized for those skills, and to be able to expand those skills is essential if we are to achieve true gender equity.

Overworking affects women's health. Part of the reason is because women have another full-time job waiting for them when they get home, and part is because of the gender inequity they experience at the office. Most of the women I know are exhausted. Women are working longer hours and carry more weight at home than men. Yet they have been taught to soldier on, working without complaint. Now that I am a woman, I see this clearly. I wish I had seen it more clearly when I was living as Paul.

When I was with the Orchard Group, our CFO was a single mother. I thought I was sensitive to her needs as a working mom. I allowed her to work flextime and gave her time off whenever she needed to attend to family matters. When she needed to have her daughter with her at work, which was rare, I was fine with it. Her daughter was a delightful child, and the truth was that I often had one of my daughters—Jana—at the office with me. (Of course, Jana was in high school, and the reason she was with me was because she was perpetually grounded, but that's a different story.) But I did not make sure our CFO was being paid what a man in her position would have been paid. I did not initiate a tuition-reimbursement program that would have paid for her master's degree. I did not do everything possible to make sure her opportunities were equal to mine. I wish I could go back and truly provide her with the support she deserved. The same is true of my executive assistant of fifteen years. She made my life so much easier. She was a brilliant woman, and I wish I had offered to pay for her ongoing education. I did not do enough to help both women who did so much to help me.

When it comes to hiring processes, there are great gender disparities. In a 2018 study of 2,106 job applications, GPA had little effect on whether or not a man would get a job. Women did well if they had a *moderately* high GPA, and less well with a *very* high GPA. High-achieving men are called back twice as often as high-achieving women. High-achieving male math majors are called back three times as often as high-achieving female math majors. Those doing the hiring value competence and commitment from male applicants, and likeability of female applicants. Moderate-achieving women are seen as more social and outgoing, while high-achieving women are viewed with more skepticism.* In other words, a woman is punished for being highly competent. Adding insult to injury, if she is hired for the job, she will be treated as if she does not know what she is talking about. She is not in your office because she is likeable. She is in your office because she is competent. Treat her accordingly.

I know the men who are reading this book are the good guys. I know you are sensitive and thoughtful, and when it comes to gender equity, you want to get it right. There is one thing you can do that will pay dividends beyond all others. Ask your wives, sisters, mothers, and daughters about their experience. Ask them what needs to change at

---

* Natasha Quadlin, "The Mark of a Woman's Record: Gender and Academic Performance in Hiring," *American Sociological Review* 83, no. 2 (March 2018).

work and at home. Listen to them. Seriously listen to them. And then do whatever you can to bring about change in your work environment.

Guys, life is tilted in your favor. Even if you do not see it, trust that what the women in your life are telling you is true. Life is more difficult for them. Leverage the power you have to create a better life for women. Create a better future for your daughters and granddaughters, and the generations to come.

I have five fierce granddaughters. They all are intelligent, are articulate, and have great emotional intelligence. All five are gifted in multiple areas. Fortunately, they are all living in environments in which they are able to receive a good education and go to excellent schools. Their socioeconomic status affords them great opportunities. But what they get from their parents goes beyond opportunities for a good education.

I love watching their fathers empower all five girls. Jael's husband, Kijana, beams when Trista lights up the room with her intelligence, thoughtfulness, and capability. She sees her own success reflected in his eyes. He encourages her interest in academics, telling her, "You can do anything you set your mind to." I love watching Tony, Jana's former husband, with the twins. He knows Ava's and Macy's strengths and is constantly encouraging them to pursue their dreams. He is a successful entrepreneur and is quick to spot their unique gifts and encourage their development and expression. I watch Jonathan with Asha and Lyla and see utter delight in his eyes as he fully takes in the unique giftedness of each daughter. What makes all three fathers so unusual is their complete devotion to empowering their daughters.

My five granddaughters also have fierce mothers. Jael and Jana work hard and excel, and they expect their daughters to work hard as well. Jubi, Jonathan's wife, has always been a high achiever, and she champions her girls, cheering them on at every turn. All three mothers are wonderful examples of women who do not take no for an answer. All three empower their daughters. With that kind of parental empowerment, I have no doubt all five girls will thrive.

Even with the extraordinary nurture and care my five granddaughters receive, it will still be more difficult for them to find success than it was for their fathers and me. Men start closer to the finish line than women. It is sad but true. Men get a head start. Until that reality changes, women will always be chasing after gender equity. If we are to achieve true gender equity, men are going to have to get to work leveling the playing field. It is the message I bring from my heart every time I step onto a podium and speak about gender equity.

CHAPTER 18

Just-in-Time Grace

The possession of knowledge does not kill the sense of
wonder and mystery. There is always more mystery.

—ANAÏS NIN

Whether it is my own journey, my desire to empower women, or my work to help men recognize and fight for gender equity, it is difficult to understand my journey without appreciating the role Christianity has played throughout my life. I am a spiritual being. My spirituality has always been dynamic, constantly changing as I have grown through various stages of faith. Those changes have quickened considerably since I transitioned. In fact, I would say they are second only to the changes in my sexuality.

As a man, my spirituality was split in half. There was one spiritual practice in my logical left brain and another in my artistic right brain. The two sides rarely spoke. My left brain approached spirituality rationally, in a manner consistent with my evangelical upbringing. *Does God exist? Is the Bible inspired by God? What is required to get into heaven?* These were the questions that occupied my left brain. My right brain was searching for beauty and harmony and found both in nature and the music I embraced, tight vocal harmonies.

My early spiritual understanding grew out of my relationship with my parents. That is true for just about all of us. I was raised within Christian evangelicalism, with a loving father and an emotionally distant mother. The majority of the obstacles I faced in developing a healthy spirituality found their genesis in my mother. I am hardly unique. For all of us, most elements of our spiritual development go back to our family of origin. When we were tiny humans, it was the big people who were apparently omnipotent and omniscient. We were well on our way to adulthood before we made the terrifying discovery that our parents had feet of clay. We could not help but project onto God our experiences at home. One particular episode explains how my view of God and the church was shaped by my family.

My mother had a habit of turning ordinary acts of affection and kindness into an opportunity to add a star to her crown. Whenever I would return to Kentucky and visit my grandmother, my mother would tell her sisters that I had no intention of visiting Grandma, but that she had forced me to see her. I was aware this was a common narrative, designed to increase my mother's standing with her sisters. Both of my aunts made me aware of it during my twenties. When I told them the truth, they were not surprised. They knew my character and how I felt about Grandma Stone. They also knew my mother played loosely with the truth. I would never have thought of visiting

Kentucky without seeing my grandmother. It bothered me to no end that my mother would tell her sisters otherwise.

When I was thirty-five, I returned to Kentucky for a short summer visit. Before I had unpacked my bags, my mother said, "You need to go see your grandmother." For the first time in my life, I stood up to her. I said, "Mom, you do not have to tell me to go see grandma. I always go." My mother turned bright red. "How dare you speak to me like that! Apologize this instant!" I said, "Mom, I have nothing for which to apologize. The truth is that you do not ever have to ask me to visit Grandma, and you know it."

Over the years when my own children have expressed frustration with me, I have always listened through to the end and usually painfully had to admit the legitimacy of what they were telling me. It's never easy, but it is essential. Good parenting demands it. It was not that way with my mother.

Not once in my life did my mother admit she had done anything wrong. She did not have the ego strength to do so. In her mind, if she admitted she was wrong, her entire house of cards would have come tumbling down. Her ability to cope was built on her shaky conviction that she was without flaw. She always responded to any disagreement with a counteraccusation. When I refused to back down, I had never seen her angrier. Mom was seething. "How dare you!"

I firmly defended myself. "Mom, I'm sorry you are so angry, but there is no reason for you to be angry. I am just telling you that I do not appreciate when you tell me to do something you already know I am going to do." Then I spoke the words that sent her over the edge. I continued, "Mom, I know you tell your sisters that I would not visit if you did not tell me to do so. It is not true, and you know good and well it is not true." With an expressionless face, she dispassionately announced, "You are no longer my child. I want you to leave!" I left and went to my aunt's house.

I know it might be hard to understand such a drastic response to my mild protestations, but that is life with a narcissistic parent. Most of the time it is easier to acquiesce than it is to stand up for yourself. My father rarely stood up to my mother. Instead, he did whatever she demanded. Early in our marriage, Cathy mentioned to my mother that it was difficult for her when I traveled for work. My mother said, "Well, you just need to forbid it." To my mother, it was that simple. You made your demands and your husband acquiesced.

My father called an hour or two after I left the house and told me I needed to apologize to my mother. He said, "You know your mother. She won't stand for this. You'll have to apologize to keep the peace." I said, "I'm done, Dad. I am not doing that anymore." With incredible sadness, the greatest I ever heard in his voice, Dad said, "Well, then, you'd better come home and pick up anything that is yours, because I am no longer your father and you are no longer my child." I knew she had walked into the room while he was speaking. I could tell by the change in his tone and shift in his language. There is no way he would have spoken those words if she had not been standing there. That was the kind of mind-bending behavior my otherwise gentle-hearted father did to remain in a marriage with her. But when he spoke those words, they hung in the air in all of their awfulness.

I did not return to Kentucky for a year. Periodically my mother would call and begin by saying, "This is your mother and I accept your apology." I would say, "Mom, I did not apologize." She would hang up. After about a year, she stopped beginning phone conversations with those words. She had learned I was going to be preaching for our denomination's national convention, and she could not keep up her charade of anger if I was going to give her such a wonderful opportunity to appropriate the accomplishments of her son. She would lie and tell her sisters I had apologized and put herself in the best position to receive the accolades she needed. As my ego grew stronger over the years, I became painfully aware of her weaknesses and motivations. My mother was a profoundly wounded woman.

I wish none of this were true. I wish I could look back and say with certainty what every child ought to be able to say—that I was unconditionally loved by the person who gave me life. But we don't all get that. And when you don't, it colors your expectations for love from all other people, and even from God. No matter how much healing you do, how strong the family you grow up to build is, or how successful you are, there is always a small voice that asks whether anyone will really love you unconditionally if the person who created you could not.

My mother's early wounding left her unable to love unconditionally. My father was loved conditionally by her, and that gave her power over him. I was loved conditionally by her, which meant I grew up without that primary sense of being loved exactly as I was.

Having grown and healed and had my own children, for whom my unconditional love sprung forth effortlessly, I am now able to look back and have great sympathy for my mother. I can only imagine how terrible her wounding must have been. On the days I believe in heaven, I have a generous theology in which I imagine my mother being in an extremely well-appointed inpatient treatment center in which she receives round-the-clock care to heal the wounds she experienced here on earth. I want my mother to have an opportunity to overcome the fears she could not overcome on this side of life.

My experiences with my parents affected my understanding of God. After my father acquiesced to my mother and disowned me, it was easy for me to continue the spiritual narrative I had created early in life—that though God might be kind and gentle, there are limits to God's love. After all, there were limits to my father's love. God is ultimately powerless in the face of an even greater power. If the church was as fickle as my mother, then I should absolutely fear the church. God was kind but powerless. The church was a stern and unreasonable taskmaster. It is ironic that when I transitioned, the church behaved exactly as my childhood had told me it would, completely rejecting me for finding the courage to be true to myself.

Yet, while my family of origin did cause me to develop an unhealthy view of God and the church, somehow I grew beyond that limited understanding and developed a more generous expression of the Christian faith that has informed and shaped every area of my life. How did that happen?

Call me an optimist, but I believe there is a holy grace at work in the world that lifts us above the outcomes one might expect based on our life experiences. I believe the majority of humans end up a good bit healthier than one might expect. I see it with my counseling clients. They tell me their horribly wounding experiences and I wonder how the clients can be as healthy as they are. What surprises me is not their wounding but the grace that has healed the wounds more quickly and completely than I would have anticipated.

The late psychiatrist and prolific author M. Scott Peck said one of the reasons he believed in God was seeing that kind of grace at work in the world. He kept having the same kinds of experiences, encountering clients who were far healthier than he would have expected. What was the source of that resilience? What was protecting these people from the worst outcomes? Peck became convinced it was the God described in the Christian scriptures. I share Peck's conviction.

I bring my generous view of grace into my work as a pastoral counselor. One of the joys I experience is seeing a client recognize goodness and grace wherever it appears in the person's life. As we work together, the client begins to see that the remarkable truth is not that terrible things happened but that those experiences did not stop them from finding their way through the darkness. At a time when they might have been overwhelmed by negative experiences, there was a powerful force at work that gave them the strength to get through those trials. I am in awe of this "just-in-time" grace.

It is important to note that I do not always see this grace at work. Sometimes a person is about as wounded as I would expect them to be. I do not know why one person receives grace, while another does not. I do know that I have been the recipient of this just-in-time grace. In so many ways, I have been blessed beyond measure, both pre- and post-transition. That blessing has resulted in a strong Christian faith, though not a conservative evangelical faith. Since I transitioned, my faith has grown deeper and broader.

When I was living as a man, I did not trust spirituality born of the heart. I wanted a reasonable faith. I focused on the question of God's existence. Could the present complexity of life have developed over a fourteen billion–year period by chance, or are we the product of intelligent design? Finding an answer to that question was important to me. Are we loved by a divine creator, or are we on our own in the world? I devoured scores of theological works. I understand why I was consumed with proving God's existence. As long as I could stay focused on something as abstract as the existence of God, I was able to stay in my head. I wanted to stay in my head. I needed to stay in my head. My heart was off-limits. There were too many open wounds in my heart. But that was not the only reason I wanted to prove whether or not God existed. When you grow up under a steady stream of exaggerations, lies, and manipulations, you tend to become a person fixated on finding fact and truth.

As I have moved through life, my faith has moved through recognizable stages. It transitioned from a magical notion of God based in imagined parental omniscience to a conventional rule-based faith, to a disenchanted time of active searching, to a re-enchanted faith, broader and more nuanced than before. I'm not sure any of that is specifically gender based, though I do see significant changes in how I perceive God and spirituality as a woman.

I love the God who burst onto the scene fourteen billion years ago in all of God's complexity and mystery and ever expansiveness, rooted in relationship and grounded in love. As the creative force of the universe, I think of God as Mother, the one who gives shape to all that exists. I also think of God as both Father and Mother, encompassing all elements of both genders. At our deepest level, we all want to embrace both our masculine and feminine sides. As a man, I struggled with my feminine side. As a woman, I spent my first several years trying to deny my masculine side. As I integrate the masculine and feminine, I am even more in awe of the mystery and expansiveness of the God who is paradoxically powerful and nurturing, sensitive and strong, light and shadow, and far beyond my ability to grasp. I pray to God spontaneously, sometimes with words, sometimes with a wonder beyond words.

Not long ago my neighbor sent everyone in the neighborhood a picture of a mother bear with her two cubs sitting on the hillside behind our homes. I printed the picture and put it on my refrigerator as a prayer. Trust me—when I was a man, I did not put pictures of bears on my refrigerator as prayers. I would have thought of it as beautiful, but nothing more. Now I see the wonder of a protective mother and her curious cubs, nurtured by the land and nearby river, living in harmony with what has been happening in this canyon for ages. I see love on a hillside redolent with nature's fall harvest, all of creation benefitting from what God set in motion. The picture tugs at my heart and touches my soul. It fills me with awe and wonder.

As a man, I thought of God as something or someone to possess. Now I think of God as someone to be possessed by. I am still a Christian and still enamored with the Jesus presented in the four Gospels. I also feel the presence of the Holy Spirit, who I experience as feminine. I see her as a gentle presence you might not think about for days but quietly feel at work within. The Spirit is what prompts my soul to slip through the cracks in the bedrock harshness of life and express its defiant, nevertheless.

The active part of my faith is centered on loving my neighbor, with the full and terrifying realization that every human being is my neighbor. It is also focused on loving myself, knowing you cannot love God or your neighbor until you love yourself. My faith is like a Rembrandt, with an infinite play of light and shadow. In fact, I have a print of Rembrandt's *Return of the Prodigal Son* on a wall of my home where I see it many times a day. I like the notion of a God who embraces both light and darkness and never stops loving two sons whose behavior is unlovely.

I used to see the church as a place for teaching theology and pondering the existence of God. Now I see it as a community of fellow travelers who do their best to love one another as God asks us to love—unconditionally. That might sound simplistic or even trite, but it is not. It is simple, but not simplistic. Since I transitioned, my life in the church has not always been easy, but it has always been good. It is where I interact with others at a similar stage on our common journey, and it is life-giving.

I am no longer obsessed with looking for theological answers and finding the right language to explain those answers. I am comfortable saying there are some things I just know. I know that while a person may live an immoral life, when they watch a movie, they want the hero to do the right thing. I no longer need to know the reason that is true. It just is. I know hate is not the opposite of love. Hate requires too much emotional energy to be the opposite of love. Apathy is the opposite of love. And above all, I know love makes the world go around. I do not need to explain that marvelous reality. I just know it.

I cannot leave a chapter about spirituality without talking about the experiences of preaching as a man and preaching as a woman. I preached often through my decades as a man. I usually spoke on the road, preaching at hundreds of churches in dozens of states and a half dozen countries. Almost all of those sermons were what I call "road sermons," generic messages designed for widely divergent audiences. I preached about the importance of taking risks, learning to fail with grace, the tendency of humans to abuse power, and the primacy of love. You might say, "That seems compatible with the spirituality you describe now." You are right. It is. That is but one example of the ways in which I am, in fact, the same person I was before I transitioned. But as with most other aspects of transitioning, there are differences in how I perceive the world now, and differences in how I preach.

Now I preach with more nuance; I speak more confessionally and more transparently. I sit with the text and listen for the whisper of God, filtered by my experience and the imagined experience of my listener. When I was a man, I was always told that my voice was masculine but gentle. I do not believe I lost much of that masculine voice when I transitioned. It has been integrated into my feminine voice. I find it fascinating that the place in which I feel the greatest continuity between Paul and Paula is when I am preaching. I wish I knew what to make of that. My friend Nicole says maybe it is because true callings are to the truest part of ourselves. I think about it every time

I preach. I watch my sermons online and see the continuity between my preaching now and my preaching when I was Paul. I am theologically freer now, which is certainly a blessing. But outside of that, and my gender, I see the same person preaching the good news of the Gospel.

When I preach, it is a flowing forth of great hope, this whispering of truth that must be known in the heart before it can be embraced by the head. And here is another truth: I know I am called to preach, as if it might be the most important thing I have remaining to do in life. I need to breathe and eat and run and love and preach. I was made to preach the Gospel of Jesus Christ. And now, finally, I can fully embrace the calling into which I was born.

The day I was ordained into the Christian ministry, my father told me for the first time why I had been named Paul. His father had requested it, wanting me to be named after the Apostle Paul, hoping another generation of Williams children would go into the ministry. Now I was living into that calling in a more meaningful way than ever before. But my father did not know that wonderful truth, because I had not seen him since I transitioned. My mother had demanded that he cut me off. I was desperate to reconnect before it was too late. My parents were both in their nineties.

I was in Phoenix on my father's ninety-third birthday and decided to give him a call at his home in Kentucky. I told him who it was that was calling, and he said, "Well, you sound different, but I can still tell it is your voice. It's good to hear from you." We had a nice thirty-minute conversation. I asked how Mom was doing in the nursing home, if he was still teaching his Sunday school class, and what he thought of his beloved Kentucky Wildcats basketball team. I didn't say much about myself. I just wanted to hear Dad talk. A few weeks later I called again and asked if I could come for a visit. He said yes and that Mom was willing to meet with me. He would do his best to see if she could be brought to the apartment from the nursing home in their assisted-living center.

In April 2016, I flew to Kentucky and had a wonderful three-hour visit with my parents. Shortly after I arrived, my mother started to express her disappointment in me, but I cut her off and said, "Mom, that's not what we are here for. We are here to visit and for me to tell you how much I love you." She accepted my words and was pleasant, if reserved, for the remainder of the visit. My conversation with my father was wonderful. We talked about all of his ministries over the years and the class he still taught at his church. I told him about my work with Highlands Church in Denver. I wanted him to know I was still preaching. Dad said, "You always have been a great preacher—my favorite, really." He had never told me that before. Dad went on to say, "You have always been as smart as a whip, too. So, when you told me you transitioned, I knew you must have a good reason. You always think things through." It meant so much to hear my father's affirming words.

As I stood to go, Dad spoke a few more words I will never forget. He said, "Paula, I do not understand this, but I am willing to try." It was the first time he called me Paula. What more could I ask? One man giving up his power because he knew what he knew—that he loved his child, and he was going to do whatever it took to honor the journey of another. It was one of the most redemptive moments of my life. Love does make the world go around.

CHAPTER 19

Religions of Hate, Religions of Love

Religion makes good people better and bad people worse.

—H. RICHARD NIEBUHR

While my Christian faith has been such an important part of my journey, it is ironic that so much of the pain I have experienced has been delivered by organized religion. How did that happen? How did something designed to soothe the soul of humankind turn into something designed to comfort the few at the expense of the many? How could evangelical Christianity move so far away from the teachings of Jesus?

I have always wanted to get it right. It is my understanding as a Christian that getting it right means loving God, loving neighbor, and loving self. It is simple, but it is not easy. Doubting everything is the beginning of wisdom. Blindly accepting the teachings of your culture might be acceptable if cultural loyalty is your heart's desire, but not if the search for truth is what energizes your soul.

For most of my working years, I was a leader in my evangelical denomination while also believing that doubting everything was the pathway to wisdom. The two were fundamentally incompatible. If I had the strength when I was younger to accept that undeniable truth, I would have left evangelicalism during my college years. But I did not. No one is an island. Few in their twenties are ready to leave the community that nurtured them, even if it is a conservative religious community.

I offer no excuses. When you are young and idealistic, you do not realize how often the compromise truck is going to pull up and offload its contents. I had a young family and wanted to be an adequate provider. I wanted the affirmation of the world in which I had been raised. Now that I am out of the evangelical subculture, it is easy to look back and ask how I could have participated in a form of Christianity with such damaging theology. But like the proverbial frog in a kettle, the boiling water of accommodation sneaks up on you. You do not realize you have sold your soul until it is too late. What was it that was so damaging about evangelical theology?

I had been taught that Christianity was a belief system, primarily propositional, that posited the notion there was a creator God who loved his creation. Unfortunately, that God was also perfect and could not stand to look at the imperfection of his creation, particularly the humans he created. His solution was to send his own son to earth to accept the punishment humans should pay for their imperfections. It was that last part that always tripped me up. From the time I was a child, it did not make sense. Would God, if he or she existed, dislike me so much that God would send me to hell? What kind of God would do that? It defied common sense. Nevertheless, a lot of smart people embrace that theology. It is the teaching known as the substitutionary atonement. Jesus was our substitute and atoned for our sins. It is one of the key teachings of fundamentalist and evangelical Christianity.

Fundamentalism is any religion that adheres to a strict, literal interpretation of its scriptures. It teaches that only the fundamentalists are the true adherents of that particular religion, and that all others are practicing a tainted version of the true faith. Christian fundamentalism and its slightly more liberal cousin, evangelicalism, teach the substitutionary atonement, that every individual must be born again so the shed blood of Jesus can serve as an atonement for our personal sins. Fundamentalists and evangelicals also believe in judgment by God after death, at which time God decides who goes to heaven and who goes to hell.

There are different types of fundamentalism. All three Abrahamic religions began as desert religions and as such were religions of scarcity. There were not enough resources to go around, so people had to take care of their own. Those three Abrahamic religions—Islam, Judaism, and Christianity—in their fundamentalist forms continue to be religions of scarcity, teaching that God's love is restricted to the elect. The elect are those within their particular branch of fundamentalism. Within each of those fundamentalist religions are innumerable subgroups, each claiming to be the only true expression of that particular religion. Fundamentalism also exists outside the boundaries of the desert religions. There are fundamentalist atheists, fundamentalist Buddhists, and fundamentalist Hindus. Wherever you have a group that judges all others to be wrong and not a part of the truly enlightened, you have a form of fundamentalism.

We are all spiritual creatures. We did not begin to thrive as a species until we began working at a level beyond blood kin. It was only when we gathered in larger communities that we began to soar. What brought us together was not the need for safety but the desire to discover the meaning of life. For what purpose are we here? And to what end? The mysteries of Stonehenge and the burial mounds of Indigenous Americans point to our desire to understand life's meaning. Spirituality is baked into our species. Fundamentalism is not.

The fundamentalist forms of the desert religions have evolved to believe an enemy is necessary for the religion to survive, and where no enemy exists, fundamentalism creates one. The current enemies created by evangelical Christians are those within the LGBTQ+ community and those who support women's rights. Should we be surprised that the two social issues chosen by these patriarchal religions are issues that personally cost their male leaders nothing? All three forms of Abrahamic fundamentalism are exclusively led by men. No male clergy have to decide whether or not to get an abortion, and fewer than 5 percent are gay or transgender. They have conveniently chosen social positions that require no sacrifice on their own part. The positions they take allow them to remain in power without having to give up any of their own comfort. Rather convenient, don't you think?

These are the same religious teachers who maintain that men are equipped by nature to lead, while women are equipped by nature to follow. They are the ones who decided women should remain silent in the church and men should be in charge. They are the religious leaders who identify enemies and plan the strategies to defeat them.

If we look at evangelical and fundamentalist Christianity, we can begin to understand the culture wars in the United States. It is difficult for those on the coasts to realize that in twenty-eight states of the United States, the major religious teaching is evangelical Christianity. It teaches that men are to be in charge of women at church, at home, and, by extrapolation, in every area of life. We underestimate the power of evangelical Christianity at our own peril. Since the 1980s evangelicals have become increasingly politically active. They began by running for positions on school boards, then demanding that those schools teach total abstinence in their sex education classes and teach a seven-day creation in science classes.

From there they began working to take over state legislatures. In a number of states, they hold the majority in both state legislative houses. They emerged onto the national scene with Tea Party Republicans and have virtually taken over the Republican Party. Seventy-six percent of evangelicals voted for Donald Trump in the 2020 election. They were more than willing to overlook his many flaws in order to get the judicial appointments they wanted. After having permeated the top levels of the legislative branch, they are wanting to leave their mark on the judicial branch, where lifetime appointments can keep their ideology in power for another generation.

Fundamentalist Christians see the Bible as a constitution, a rule book designed to govern the way people live. They are originalists, seeing the Bible as a document that should be interpreted according to its understanding at the time it was written. Over the centuries it has caused fundamentalists and evangelicals to teach that the sun revolves around the earth, that slavery is acceptable, and that the world was created in seven twenty-four-hour days. They have taught that divorce and remarriage will cause a person to fall out of favor with God, that transracial families are unacceptable to God, and that LGBTQ+ people are going to hell.

Seeing the Bible as a rule book serves no one except the men who enforce the rules. If you believe the "right" interpretation of the Bible, as defined by your male religious leaders, you will go to heaven. Believe the "wrong" interpretation and you will go to hell.

How do people escape from the toxic bubble of fundamentalism?

Religious roots run deep, and it is easy to become entangled in a toxic faith. When my children were young, Jonathan teased his sisters mercilessly. For the better part of a decade, he taught Jana that her left was her right and her right was her left. Cathy and I never knew this academy of deceit was playing out in the family room on Saturday mornings while we were asleep. Jana still has difficulty telling her right from her left. That is what fundamentalism does. It teaches you left is right and right is left, and as long as you stay in that insular environment, you accept those instructions as the gospel truth.

If you grow up in that kind of insular culture, the notion that a loving father would send his children to hell starts to make sense. But for those of us who are terminally curious, there comes a time when your doubt forces its way through the cardboard walls of your flimsy theology. Eventually, you cannot help but question the narrative of the fatherland. I see it with clients all the time. They come to me for counseling because they know I found the courage to leave evangelicalism, and they want to find the courage to do the same. I tell them it is a long and arduous journey, full of pain and loss. Some choose not to continue; the price is too high. Those who show up to do the work have an uncommon courage I greatly admire.

It takes a brave heart to leave the cocoon of conservative religion. Long, cold nights are spent in the desert while the lights of home beckon. You cannot go back. If you do return and walk through the door, you realize it is no longer home, no longer a place that is expecting you. It might be expecting a less mature you, but not the one that walks through the door. You know too much for it to ever be home again. You wonder if you will always be a nomad, wandering the desert. You question why you left, while those who slept in the bunk bed above you are still snuggled by the fire, content in the confines of their childhood home.

The truth is that you could not stay. You had to leave. You found the courage to abandon the toxic narrative that was holding you back. You allowed your mind to take in new information and transform you. You found the courage to take the road less traveled by because you understood that religion has always been and always will be evolving, and there have been many who have come before who have traveled a courageous path similar to yours.

What kind of a Christianity did I end up embracing? I gravitated toward a generous expression of Christianity. Instead of focusing on right beliefs, I have a faith that focuses on right practice. I understand Christianity as primarily loving God, loving neighbor, and loving self.

Instead of God being an angry judge who sends people to hell, I understand God as the ultimate suffering participant, showing solidarity with us in our suffering. I embrace the God who comes to earth in the form of Jesus and says, "I know life is hard, but I will walk every step of the way with you, including through the valley of the shadow of death."

Nonpatriarchal Christianity does not see the church as existing for its own self-protection but as existing for the common good. One group that has led the way in this shift is the Franciscans, a Roman Catholic order that for centuries has been teaching that God is the ultimate loving servant, not the angry taskmaster. That message of generous Christianity has a long history with the church mothers, going all the way back to Mary Magdalene, one of the closest disciples of Jesus, and extending to Brigid of Kildare, Julian of Norwich, Teresa of Ávila, Thérèse of Lisieux, Catherine of Siena, and twentieth-century leaders like Dorothy Day and Mother Teresa.

Whether it is Christianity, Islam, or Judaism, we can only hope that the more generous expressions of the desert religions will have greater influence going forward, as we envision a world in which we no longer create enemies who do not exist, but work together to secure the health of the planet and our species.

When it comes to the possibilities of religion, I am an optimist. I share the sentiments of the great theologian Pierre Teilhard de Chardin, who wrote, "Someday, after mastering the winds, the waves, the tides and gravity, we shall harness for God the energies of love, and then, for a second time in the history of the world, man will have discovered fire."*

* Pierre Teilhard de Chardin, *The Evolution of Chastity*, as translated by René Hague in *Toward the Future* (New York: Harcourt, Inc., 1975).

CHAPTER 20

Gender and Sexuality

*Love's mysteries in souls do grow, but yet the body
is his book.*

—JOHN DONNE

As a transgender person, I never welcomed the arrival of testosterone. I did not go through puberty until I was fifteen, and from the time I first experienced an unrequested sexual response, I was not happy. Why was blood rushing to that part of my body? Why was it no longer easy for me to have a girl as a friend without also fantasizing about having sex with her? It was inconsistent with who I felt myself to be. I was not a boy, I was a girl, and feeling indiscriminate male sexual desire was not something I welcomed. My teen years were a time of sexual confusion and frustration. I know what you are thinking: *Welcome to the human race*. But it is especially frustrating when your sexuality is not discussed in any sex-ed course, and you are in an evangelical family. Everything I learned about sexuality was by trial and error, and all of it was governed by the strict evangelical teaching that sexual intercourse before marriage was wrong.

After Cathy and I married, I quickly discovered how deeply I enjoyed our sexual intimacy. In all the years I was dating, I had an ongoing dilemma. I would be attracted to a girl, but I also wanted to be the girl to whom I was attracted. It had never been that way with Cathy. I did not want to be her; I just wanted to be with her. Sexual intimacy was a point of strong connection throughout our marriage. It brought the abiding intimacy for which I had been longing. Yet as I have written, it was also accompanied by a sad knowing that because I was in the wrong body, sexual intimacy was not everything I wanted it to be.

When I transitioned, I was eager to see the differences in how I would experience my sexuality. To talk about those differences, I have to begin with the aspects of male sexuality with which I always struggled. No matter how much I did not want it to be that way, when I was a man, sex was too focused on about ten seconds of the lovemaking experience. You know, *that* ten seconds. My body was far more focused on sexual release than I wanted it to be. I wanted sex to be about intimacy and closeness, and sometimes it was. But far too often my body had different ideas.

Spirituality and sexuality are closely intertwined. If you think about it, what is the universal phrase spoken at the time of sexual climax? Regardless of language or ethnic group or age or gender, the most common phrase is some variation of "Oh God!" The part of our being that wants oneness with God is the same part that wants oneness with another human. To have testosterone hijack that desire and make it about sexual release was frustrating. It separated my sexuality from my spirituality. For me, that was the most difficult aspect of sex as a man.

My sexuality as a woman is very different. It is no longer about that ten seconds. It is about the other twenty-three hours, fifty-nine minutes, and fifty seconds. Have we connected through the day? Has there been tenderness and affection? Is there a strong emotional connection? It does not always have to be a happy connection. It can include disagreement and conflict, but within the bond of love. Intimacy can be a way to come together when words are difficult to find. It can heal and mend and reset the conversation, an intimacy beyond language.

When I was Paul, my sexuality was a driving force, but to its own end. It was always disturbing to me just how much my sexuality was focused on sexual climax. It was like ignoring the appetizer, salad, and main course, because all I could think about was the dessert. My male sexuality confused me. From the day during my teens when it announced its full arrival to the day I transitioned, sex was a problem.

I have no doubt that some of my inability to enjoy my male sexuality had more to do with being raised as an evangelical than being transgender. Evangelicalism teaches that normal sexual desire is sin. Masturbation is sin. Lust, sexual feelings toward anyone other than your spouse, is sin. And above all else, having sex before marriage is sin. To arrive on your wedding night as anything other than a virgin is to guarantee an eternity in hell. The evangelical notion of sexual purity was absurdly restrictive, an artificial stricture that had nothing to do with the teachings of Jesus and everything to do with clergy maintaining control over the flock. If you could convince people that the most basic human desire is something sinful, and you were the only one able to forgive those sins, you could pretty much guarantee retaining your power.

Linda Kay Klein's wonderful book, *Pure*, describes the damage done by the evangelical purity movement. Even if you were married, evangelicalism made the enjoyment of intimacy difficult. You brought all of those feelings of shame into the marriage with you.

There is no question I was negatively affected by evangelical teaching about sex. My father's steadfast avoidance of the subject was another problem. He never said a single word about sexuality to me—not one word. About a year after my first sexual experience, my mother tried to explain what masturbation was, but it was a conversation that was so wrong at so many levels. First, what teenage boy wants to hear his mother say anything at all about sex, let alone about masturbation? Second, to hear her tell it, sex was for procreation and nothing else. She always referred to sex as the "devil's playground." When I was a kid, I thought, *If hell is such an awful place, then why does it have a playground?* I mean, was there recess in hell? Did you join Sisyphus pushing rocks up a hill until the bell rang for recess, when the rocks rolled back down again, but you got to go have sex? If that was the case, well, I could imagine worse.

Suffice it to say, I was not prepared for sexual intimacy. Add being transgender to that, and it was pretty much guaranteed that my sexual experience in marriage was going to have a steep learning curve. It helped that Cathy and I learned together. Our devotion to each other carried us through. I suppose the silver lining was that Cathy and I thought we were the first people on earth to discover many of the joys of sex. We learned by experimentation, and desire, and the openness we both had to expanding our horizons.

Would my sexual experience as a man have been better if I had not been raised in the evangelical world? I am sure it would have, but it would not have changed the fact that male sexuality never felt right to me. Just as I always knew I should have been born a girl, I also knew I should be experiencing sex as a woman, not as a man.

Sexual identity and gender identity are not synonymous. Sexual identity is who you want to go to bed with. Gender identity is who you want to go to bed as. I am still attracted to cisgender women, as I have always been, but my sexuality is less visual and more holistic than when I was a man. Back then, much of my sexual focus was visual. Now my sexuality is about all of my senses. It is especially about touch. When I was a man, my love languages were acts of service and words of affirmation. Now I would add physical touch to the list. It does not have to be specifically sexual touch. All physical touch is sexual touch.

As a woman, I am far more aware of the energy emanating from another person than I was when I was a man. In fact, if you asked when I was a man, "Do you feel energy from another person's body?" I would have looked at you quizzically and said, "Don't get all 'woo-woo' on me!" I had never experienced anything like that. Now it happens frequently. I would describe it as a warmth or even a spirit that emanates from the other person. I accept its existence as a mystery, even a wonder.

My sexual expression is connected to every part of the relationship. There is one single whole, a relationship that is sexual, spiritual, and somatic. Sexually, I am attracted to women, as I have always been. Spiritually, my sexuality is uncoupled from the teachings of evangelicalism and integrated into every part of me. Somatically, I am finally in the body I always knew I was supposed to have—a soft, feminine body.

When I was a guy, Cathy's hand on my back, a kiss goodbye as I headed out the door, a welcoming embrace—none of it registered as much more than something couples do in the course of a day. I took it for granted, and it did not result in strong sexual desire. There were things Cathy could do that would get me in the mood, but they were direct and, in retrospect, stereotypically male. If she wore tight jeans, a low-cut blouse, or high heels, I took notice. If she was brushing her hair in the morning or stepping out of the shower, I was interested. If she was fixing breakfast, singing a song, or playing with the kids in the backyard, my desire was on high alert. If she used specifically sexual language, I was right there. There was a direct connection between the way she looked and sexual desire. My desire was lit by two of the five senses—sight and sound. The other three did not play much of a role. When we were making love, all five senses finally showed up. But as soon as my body had done its thing, it was like the back side of a fast-moving hurricane. The winds shifted, and before you knew it, they were gone.

Now the lightest touch of a hand on my face, and you have my attention. To hold the face of a beloved in the palms of my hands is heavenly. Intimacy is facing each other with our backs against the armrests of the couch as we talk about the day. It is looking at the clock after a long, deep conversation and saying to each other, "Surely it can't be that late. It felt like minutes."

It's holding each other tightly when we are afraid, knowing that one embrace will carry us through the night. It is giving each other flowers, because who doesn't love a fresh bouquet on the kitchen counter reminding you that love abides? It is ordinary moments that become extraordinary, just because of the look you give each other across a crowded room. It is treasuring the love that flows out of one quick glance.

Intimacy is knowing the dark corners of the heart of the beloved, the ones no one has been allowed to see, and knowing just the right moment to touch the heart in that sacred, wounded place. It is delighting in the otherness of the beloved and taking pleasure in saying from your heart, "You get to do you." It is knowing when it is time to fight, and when it is time to extend grace. It is risking love, knowing there is no love without pain and loss. It is knowing that even if intimacy ends, there will still be love, persistent, heartfelt, and abiding. It is understanding there are times to pull close and times to let go and trusting your soul to know which one is needed in each holy moment.

It's writing your own card instead of looking for a card with the right words already in it, which you can never find because they are never your words. It is knowing where that handwritten card will be kept and how often it will be read.

Intimacy is breast touching breast, hearts aligned, and love kindled. It is the precious knowing of feminine love, rich in passion, sealed with a soft touch. It holds lightly to the beloved, understanding that the greater you love, the lighter you hold your beloved. It leaves room for the Spirit, and the reasons of two hearts, intertwined like the branches of a tree that has learned to yield to the wind.

It is staying in the moment of the first touch, the one you did not even know was the most intimate of places, that had always been waiting to be brought to life. Intimacy is not trying to prove anything. It is taking pleasure in the moment. Every sense is present, even the senses beyond the senses, the ones that fill the air with an otherworldly gentleness born of delight. The feelings you cannot describe, that keep you in the moment, gripped by the invisible energy of feminine love, the sisterhood of knowing.

There is no hurry to intimacy, no beginning or end, just a suspension of what will be taken up again in the tender moment after a glance across the room that is its own invitation. It stays in the space around you, like that favorite sweater that has the power to warm you just by thinking about it draped around your shoulders. Intimacy is born of the pain of knowing what women know, that loving greatly always has a price, and the price is knowing a piece of your heart will be left in every heart you have ever loved, just as a piece of that person's heart remains in you, never to be lost because if it were, you might lose your own soul.

It is knowing we are made of the intangible connections of mothers and daughters and women through the generations who have known in their hearts what all women know, that love makes the world turn and is the ground of all good things.

Intimacy is warm blankets, and sunflowers, and bacon in the morning because sometimes you have to have bacon. It is ripe tomatoes in a summer salad from the garden you worked together with your tender hands. It is the soft light from a distant room that brings pleasure to your eyes and the outline of curves to trace with your sensitive fingers. It is an intimacy born of similarity, a closeness that comes from touching the familiar, but the familiar as wholly and holy other. It is love from the heart and soul and the places beneath the places.

It is love born of a kindred knowing, a common touch, aligned hearts and souls that know the Spirit is always present, even if you don't feel her for days. It is as steady as a warm breeze, as bracing as a mountain stream, and as fleeting as the golden days of fall that remind you there is nothing more beautiful than this planet and every living thing on it, especially your beloved and especially you.

Intimacy is spending the day lying in the grass because what else should you have done? Watching the trees in the wind telling you their stories of a lifetime together in just one place, branch touching branch. If you listen closely, they will tell you their names.

It is sitting on the patio in the warmth of the sun, listening to her chuckle because you just looked up and announced to no one in particular that a British Aerospace 146 just flew overhead, but you have no idea it is a red-tailed hawk that just landed on your fence. You had to ask its name.

Intimacy is hope in a silhouette at dawn, after your nightmares have frightened you into believing that true love is an illusion. It is touching that silhouette ever so lightly and knowing the love you share is not an illusion but a thing of beauty you did not even know could be known.

My sexuality is extraordinary and holy and full of joy because it is *my* sexuality, the sexuality of the body I now inhabit, the one I was supposed to have been born with, the one that brings me pleasure in ways I did not know there was pleasure to be known.

And one last thing. Like every other part of being transgender, I speak from the borderlands between genders. I have no illusions that my sexuality is the same as the sexuality of a cisgender woman. It is the sexuality of a transgender woman, and not just any transgender woman but the one who is writing this memoir.

Of all the changes that have taken place since I transitioned, the changes in my sexuality are the greatest. I talk to God about it. You know, the God who is both male and female and therefore understands. God answers, "Yes, I do understand. What you knew as a man was wonderful. What you know as a woman is wonderful. They are both beautiful expressions of what it means to be human." But I say, "Yes, but God, let's talk about female sexuality, and let's be honest. Isn't that what you really had in mind?" God answers, "Well, Paula, if you had been comfortable as a man, you might have felt differently. But you're transgender, my dear, and that has given you a very unique perspective. Enjoy what sex feels like in both genders. I certainly do."

CHAPTER 21

For the Greater Good

Last night as I was sleeping, I dreamt—marvelous
error!—that I had a beehive here inside my heart. And
the golden bees were making white combs and sweet
honey from my old failures.

—ANTONIO MACHADO, "LAST NIGHT AS I WAS SLEEPING"

I was warming a cup of tea when it slipped from my hand, shattering on the kitchen floor. The cup, a Cath Kidston mug, was one of my favorites. I own a dozen Cath Kidston mugs, but this was my only blue mug. It reminded me of my grandmother's china. I love a cup of Irish breakfast tea in the morning, and the Cath Kidston mugs hold a full sixteen ounces. I like the feel of them in my hand. That particular style is no longer available. When the mug shattered, I cried so

235

hard I could barely catch my breath. I wept as I swept up the pieces and carefully placed every last speck of stoneware on a dinner plate. I placed the plate, holding its stoneware, on the dresser in my bedroom, awaiting a miracle. I do not cry easily. Throughout my life I have needed prompting to bring me to tears. Movies are reliable at drawing out my emotions, but to the best of my knowledge, this was the first time tears flowed on account of breaking stoneware.

My life is difficult. Yours is, too—I know. Life is not easy for any of us. Those we love slip through our fingers, and we are shattered. When you choose to love someone, you are also choosing grief and loss, because even a lifelong love is eventually lost, either from your own death or the passing of the beloved.

Life includes a steady stream of losses. We lose the warmth of the womb, and the hearth of home. We lose the joy of tucking our children into bed and after that, our precious grandchildren. We lose the parents we love and the memories they take with them. And finally, we lose ourselves before we ever really find ourselves. We have hopes for what lies beyond the grave, but they are the substance of things hoped for and the evidence of things not seen.

If you are wise, you trust life's flow. Like the river that runs through the town where I live, my life's flow was interrupted by a great flood of biblical proportions that changed the landscape not only for me, but also for those I love. For everyone, there was a great shattering. As our family's ground was shaken, the myth of certainty was exposed. Everything we assumed our family would always be was gone. Courage and bravery were called forth as we gave up the notion of life as a predictable narrative and embraced it as a series of difficult choices, with nothing to guide us but love.

Joy and happiness are not synonymous. Happiness comes pretty much when you expect it. You get a promotion, you are happy. You get a bigger tax return than you expected, you are happy. I have known great happiness in my life, both before and after my transition. Happiness comes when you expect it. Joy has a mind of its own. Even in the midst of great trials, you can be surprised by joy. It arrives as the faintest whiff of an oasis in the desert, a thing of wonder in an unexpected place. Joy is not overpowering. It comes as a whisper.

Joy arrives in the middle of a counseling session, when a client makes a breakthrough they have been working on for years. It comes when you are talking with someone you love at 9:00 on a Saturday night and she cannot see her way through great pain, and you realize you know how to help her, and you do. Joy is when a relationship you thought had been lost returns to life, wounded, but somehow deeper and more abiding.

You experience joy when you discover a poet whose words bring that most elusive of gifts, insight. It comes when your granddaughter says, "I love being at your house, GramPaula." It was a moment of great joy when Jonathan's girls announced that henceforth and forevermore, I would be known as GramPaula. The rest of my granddaughters took to it quickly, though Trista had already christened me Paula Blossom, a name so precious I can hardly stand it.

Joy comes when you are able to comfort your former wife in her moment of grief, because usually you can't. You are too much the cause of that grief. Joy arrives with love, the kind you thought you might never know in your new body. And like all loves, it is tender and tenuous and vulnerable, but still, it is joy.

There is no way through the desert but forward. Fear makes you want to go back. Happiness makes you want to stand still. But joy calls you forward. I can understand how Odysseus felt when he finally returned to Ithaca and his beloved Penelope, only to discover that he was called to go on yet one last journey. That is my life. When

I transitioned, I thought I had returned home to Ithaca. I could finally rest. But it was not to be. There was another call I could not refuse, the call to keep moving forward through the desert, to lessen the suffering of others, to speak about gender inequity, transgender acceptance, religious tolerance, and the hero's journey. It is all summed up in a line I inserted into my first TEDx Talk the night before I spoke, a line I used again when Jonathan and I spoke for TEDWomen, a line I have used multiple times in this memoir: "The call toward authenticity is sacred and holy and for the greater good."

Where do I go from here? I have no idea. We are never sure about these things. Life unfolds as we move forward through the desert, one foot in front of the other. I live alone in my home in the foothills of the Rockies. At night the house creaks and snaps and groans and reminds me there are no firm foundations in this space between two great mysteries. Everything is temporary and everyone we know shall pass. But I move forward, waiting for a whiff of the next oasis.

Cathy lives twenty-five minutes away. We see each other every week when she comes to see clients in the office we share at the house we built together. I continue my pastoral counseling practice. I love working with my clients as each one heroically moves forward on his or her own holy and sacred journey. I serve as a co-pastor at a church in Boulder County, Colorado, doing the work I was made to do, preaching the good news that we are all in this together, and that love wins.

I wrote in my blog about the shattering of my blue Cath Kidston mug. I told my readers it was no longer in production and I had spent quite a while searching for a replacement but finally gave up. A few weeks later, a large box was delivered to the building in which our church meets. Inside, wrapped in a mile of Bubble Wrap, was the same blue Cath Kidston mug. One of my readers had found it in a

British store and had it sent to me. A few weeks later another identical mug arrived from a second thoughtful reader.

That is my life. Yes, I get hate mail, but I also have anonymous friends who search far and wide for the blue Cath Kidston mug that reminds me of my grandmother's china. One of the new mugs is in my kitchen. I gave Cathy the second one. She told me it is her favorite mug.

And the original mug on my bedroom dresser? It is there still, all the broken pieces on the dinner plate where I first placed them the day the mug shattered. The broken mug has been replaced by two perfect ones, but my favorite mug in the whole house is the shattered one on my bedroom dresser. The miracle is grasping the truth that something shattered can be a thing of beauty.

To all who believe the call toward authenticity is sacred and holy and for the greater good, there are no guarantees you will find happiness, but you will know joy.

Acknowledgments

I am indebted to the many good souls who helped me complete this memoir. I owe special thanks to my agent, Roger Freet, for his wisdom and guidance. I am grateful to everyone at Simon & Schuster for making this a seamless and enjoyable experience. I am especially thankful for my editor, Michelle Herrera Mulligan, who knew when to push and when to comfort. Carla Godwin and Jenny Martin offered thoughtful feedback to early drafts. Nicole Vickey found most of the epigraphs at the beginning of each chapter. She also read every draft and never let me settle for less than my best. Kristie Sykes propped up my courage and graciously listened as I read the manuscript aloud. Special thanks to David Reynolds for the late evening phone calls, and to Nicole, Kristie, and John, my co-pastors at Left Hand Church, for giving me the time I needed to complete the manuscript. Finally, I thank Cathy, Jonathan, Jael, Jana, Jubi, and Kijana for their love and grace as we made our way through the dark night all the way to dawn.

About the Author

Dr. Paula Stone Williams is an internationally known speaker on gender equity, LGBTQ+ advocacy, and religious tolerance. She is a pastor and pastoral counselor in Boulder County, Colorado.